ISSUE NO. 270

U.S. Department of Justice
Office of Justice Programs
National Institute of Justice

I0448455

NIJ

National Institute of Justice

JOURNAL

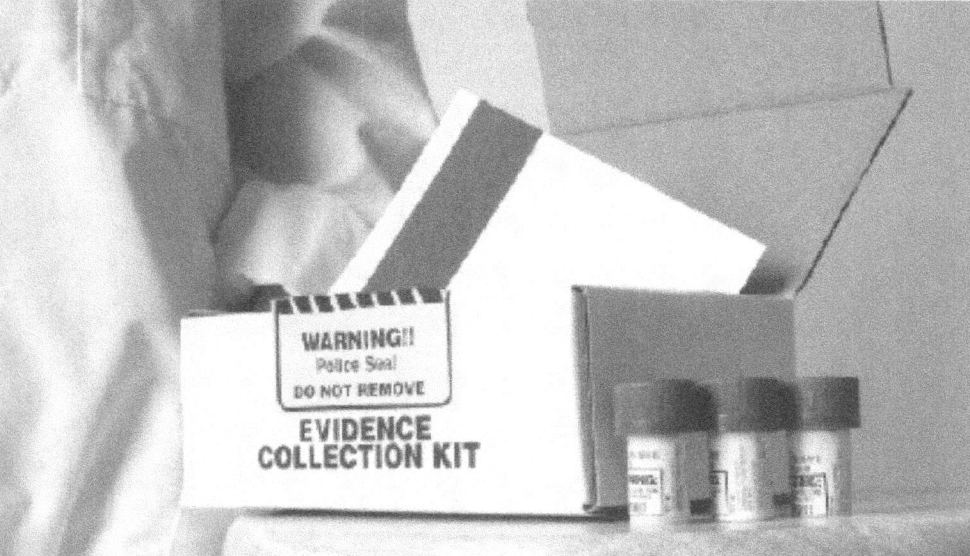

WARNING!!
Police Seal
DO NOT REMOVE
EVIDENCE
COLLECTION KIT

Solving Sexual Assaults: Finding Answers Through Research

- Collecting DNA From Arrestees: Implementation Lessons

- To Err Is Human: Using Science to Reduce Mistaken Eyewitness Identifications in Police Lineups

- In Search of a Job: Criminal Records as Barriers to Employment

Also in this issue

Preventing Children's Exposure to Violence: The Defending Childhood Initiative

Sleep Disorders, Work Shifts and Officer Wellness

The Economist's Guide to Crime Busting

U.S. Department of Justice
Office of Justice Programs

810 Seventh St. N.W.
Washington, DC 20531

Eric H. Holder, Jr.
Attorney General

Mary Lou Leary
Acting Assistant Attorney General

John H. Laub
Director, National Institute of Justice

This and other publications and products of the National Institute of Justice can be found at:

National Institute of Justice
http://www.nij.gov

Office of Justice Programs
Innovation • Partnerships • Safer Neighborhoods
http://www.ojp.usdoj.gov

NCJ 238482

BUILDING
KNOWLEDGE TO
MEET THE CHALLENGE OF
CRIME AND JUSTICE

National Institute of Justice

John H. Laub
Director, National Institute of Justice

The *NIJ Journal* is published by the National Institute of Justice to announce the Institute's policy-relevant research results and initiatives. The Attorney General has determined that publication of this periodical is necessary in transacting the public business of the U.S. Department of Justice as required by law.

Findings and conclusions of the research reported here are those of the authors and do not necessarily reflect the official position or policies of the U.S. Department of Justice.

All products, manufacturers and organizations cited in this publication are presented for informational purposes only, and their discussion does not constitute product approval or endorsement by the U.S. Department of Justice.

Subscription Information
Online   https://puborder.ncjrs.gov/Listservs/nij/reg.asp
Phone   301-519-5500
            800-851-3420
Mail   NCJRS
            P.O. Box 6000
            Rockville, MD 20849-6000

World Wide Web Address
http://www.nij.gov/journals/welcome.htm

Contact NIJ
National Institute of Justice
810 Seventh St. N.W., Washington, DC 20531, USA
http://www.nij.gov/about/contact.htm

NIJ Journal Editorial Board
Thomas E. Feucht
Lee Mockensturm
Angela Moore
Marilyn Moses
Nancy Ritter
Kristina Rose
George Tillery
Cheryl Crawford Watson

Editor-in-Chief
Jolene Hernon

Contact the Managing Editor
sberson@palladianpartners.com

Production
Palladian Partners, Inc.

Sarah B. Berson, *Managing Editor*
Amy Schneider, *Production Editor*
Aaron Auyeung, *Designer*
Maureen Berg, *Designer*

Director's Message

As this issue of the *NIJ Journal* goes to press, I am approaching my two-year anniversary as NIJ Director. I could use a number of words to describe my experience — *challenging, rewarding, frustrating* and *fulfilling* are some that come to mind. Upon my arrival, I set forth 10 goals for the Institute. We have made progress toward many of these goals while facing challenges in others. Despite these challenges, we endeavor to reaffirm NIJ's commitment to science. Although all of our goals and related efforts are important, I want to highlight three.

Establish NIJ as the leader in science-based research on crime and justice

I have placed a major emphasis on translational criminology, which seeks to bridge the gap between research, policy and practice. NIJ is thinking hard about how to translate and disseminate its research findings. We launched several initiatives that will help NIJ establish itself as the leader in science-based crime and justice research. These include a new Office of Research Partnerships that will build relationships; leverage resources; and initiate, manage and coordinate internal and external partnerships.

Create an organizational culture grounded in science and research

We have taken steps toward creating an organizational culture grounded in science and research. For example, we have hired Dr. Greg Ridgeway as a new Senior Executive Service-level Deputy Director to oversee NIJ's three science offices. Having a high-quality scientist in this key leadership position is essential for institutionalizing science at NIJ. In addition, we piloted several standing peer-review panels to strengthen our review processes and put it on par with those of other highly respected federal science agencies. We also breathed new life into our Visiting Fellows Program and started an Executive Fellows Program.

Obtain more money for social science research, and achieve integration between the physical, forensic and social sciences

Though budget challenges loom large, we have made some progress toward our goal of obtaining more money for social science research. In fiscal year 2012, we have a 2 percent budget set aside to spend on research and statistics priorities with our sister agency, the Bureau of Justice Statistics (BJS). BJS and NIJ have launched several new projects, including mining administrative police records for statistical and research purposes and examining the victim-offender overlap. In addition, NIJ is developing research portfolios in new areas, including desistance from crime, race and victimization, and indigent defense.

In terms of integrating the three bedrock sciences at NIJ, we have made some significant advancement. For example, we have a number of joint projects focusing on law enforcement officer safety, evaluation of police strategies and crime mapping, which draw on the physical and social sciences. We also have an active program of research on social science and forensic science.

Although we have accomplished much in meeting our goals, there is still work to be done. I welcome your suggestions on how NIJ can improve its efforts, especially with regard to outreach and research dissemination to you — our stakeholders.

John H. Laub
Director, National Institute of Justice

Visit the NIJ Director's page at http://www.nij.gov/about/director.

NIJ

June 2012
NIJ JOURNAL / ISSUE NO. 270

Contents

Publications
IN BRIEF

DNA for the Defense Bar

NIJ's *DNA for the Defense Bar* is the fourth publication in a collection created to provide the criminal justice field with the most up-to-date information about DNA and how it can be used in the courtroom. Specifically designed as a resource for criminal defense attorneys, *DNA for the Defense Bar* was produced by a multidisciplinary working group with oversight by the National Clearinghouse for Science, Technology and the Law at Stetson University College of Law.

Topics covered include:

- The biology of DNA
- Proper collection procedures for DNA evidence

- Interpretation of DNA analysis and findings
- When and why an expert is needed
- Development of case theory in a DNA-based prosecution or a case in which there should be DNA evidence
- Legal issues for pretrial and trial in cases with DNA evidence
- Postconviction cases

▶ Look for this publication on NIJ.gov later this summer.

Public Safety Bomb Suit Standard and Certification Program Requirements

Ensuring the safety of law enforcement officers is among NIJ's top priorities. To address the safety needs of bomb technicians, NIJ recently released the *Public Safety Bomb Suit Standard* (NIJ Standard-0117.00). This voluntary standard addresses subjects ranging from foot protection to blast overpressure. Experienced practitioners, technical experts and proper testing contributed to the development of the standard.

NIJ also released the *Public Safety Bomb Suit Standard Certification Program Requirements* (NIJ CR-0117.00), which provides the latest information on how to receive and retain accreditation. It also includes the International Organization for Standardization/International Electrotechnical Commission Guide 65 requirements.

The program requirements in this document help ensure that manufacturers and suppliers of bomb suits adhere to the *Public Safety Bomb Suit Standard.*

Both publications are available on NCJRS.gov:

- *Public Safety Bomb Suit Standard,* https://ncjrs.gov/pdffiles1/nij/227357.pdf
- *Public Safety Bomb Suit Standard Certification Program Requirements,* https://ncjrs.gov/pdffiles1/nij/237910.pdf

▶ See Tom Sharkey of the National Bomb Squad Advisory Committee wearing a bomb suit at the 2011 NIJ Conference, and learn more about standards development at NIJ, at http://nij.ncjrs.gov/multimedia/video-nijconf2011-stoe-sharkey-bailor.htm.

News & Notes

NIJ and Australia Partner on Forensics

NIJ Director John Laub and National Institute of Forensic Science Director Alastair Ross signed a memorandum of understanding (MOU) to join forces in the area of forensics.

The MOU gives the United States and Australia an opportunity to combine their research and development efforts in evaluating and using new forensic technologies.

"I continue to believe in the multiplying force of such partnerships to spark scientific synergy and creativity," stated Laub.

This is NIJ's second MOU on forensic science; the first was with the Netherlands.

▶ Read more at www.nij.gov/nij/about/director/australian-mou.htm.

Deterrence and the Death Penalty

Current research is not useful in determining whether capital punishment is less or more effective as a deterrent than alternative punishments, such as a life sentence without the possibility of parole. This finding is from a new report from the National Research Council. The report was funded in part by NIJ.

▶ Learn more at http://www8.nationalacademies.org/onpinews/newsitem.aspx?RecordID=13363.

Newest Research Findings

Examining Kansas' 123 Bill

While other states were repealing mandatory prison sentences for simple drug possession, Kansas was creating mandatory probation sentences. Kansas Senate Bill 123 (SB 123), signed into law in 2003, requires mandatory community-based supervision and substance abuse treatment for nonviolent individuals convicted of a first or second offense of drug possession.

Researchers conducted a study to evaluate the effectiveness of this bill. The study examined the bill's impact on the following:

- Diversion, recidivism and prison populations
- Sentencing practices and sentence lengths
- Supervision practices and interactions across criminal justice agencies

The results from the research showed that SB 123 improved the lines of communication between agencies. For example, SB 123 helped promote a team approach between supervising officers, drug treatment providers and probationers. However, the research also showed that SB 123 diverted few individuals from prison at sentencing, had no impact on recidivism rates relative to other community-based sanctions and had a minimal impact on prison populations. During the first three years, the bill reduced admissions to prison by diverting between 122 and 214 prison-bound individuals at sentencing. The researchers concluded that the minimal impact of SB 123 resulted from structural aspects of the law, including narrow eligibility requirements and mandatory sentencing and supervision procedures.

▶ Read the full report at http://www.ncjrs.gov. Keyword: NCJ 238012.

Violence Against Women: Special Issue on the Criminal Justice Response to Sexual Violence

This collection features four articles by preeminent researchers deeply involved in partnerships with practitioners working in the field. The introduction by guest editors Bethany Backes, a social science analyst at NIJ, and Catherine McNamee, a program analyst at the Bureau of Justice Assistance, describes the research investment made by NIJ to increase the capabilities of law enforcement and forensic science to provide victims with just outcomes and hold offenders accountable.

Since 2001, NIJ has supported research that helps inform and improve criminal justice practice and response. In 2008, the Institute held a workshop that brought researchers, service providers and forensic experts together to discuss sexual violence. The workshop helped direct NIJ's focus to three major areas: multidisciplinary responses, forensics and criminal justice responses. A detailed summary of the workshop is available at http://www.nij.gov/topics/crime/violence-against-women/workshops/sexual-violence-research.htm.

▶ Read abstracts from the issue at http://vaw.sagepub.com/content/18/2.toc (full issue available to subscribers).

.gov

Look for multimedia links throughout this issue of the *NIJ Journal*. On the NIJ website, look for the following new content:

▶ New corrections technology pages

▶ Body armor videos for officers and purchasing agents

▶ Redonna Chandler discussing how drugs affect the brain and what we know about evidence-based treatment options

▶ Janet Lauritsen discussing findings from the National Crime Victimization Survey

▶ Updates to John Laub's "Director's Corner"

▶ NIJ FY2012 grant solicitations and information about past awards

▶ Current training opportunities

▶ Past issues of the *NIJ Journal*

http://www.nij.gov

Go to NIJ.gov and subscribe to our email alerts to receive the latest information on funding, publications, trainings, events and topical pages.

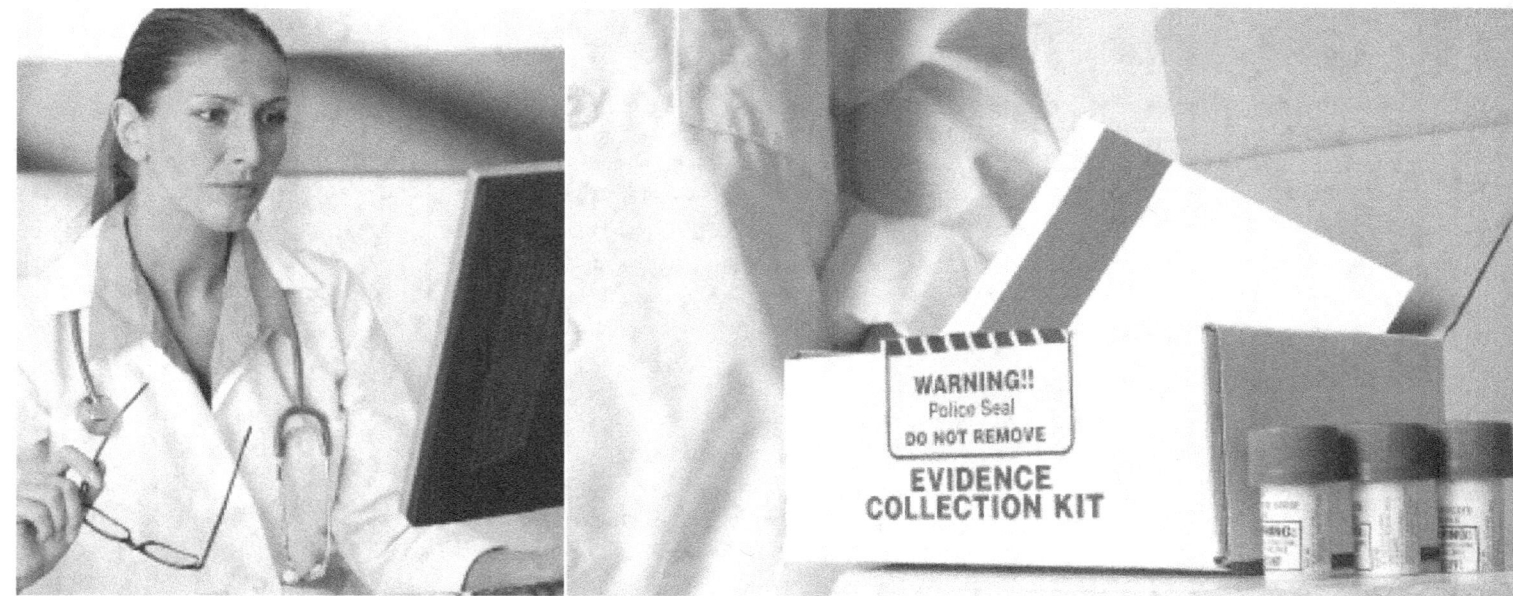

Solving Sexual Assaults:
Finding Answers Through Research

by Nancy Ritter

Research on DNA testing sexual assault kits reveals a complex picture.

It has been a headline-making story for the past few years: thousands of sexual assault evidence kits — untested — in police storage. In a few jurisdictions, lawmakers have responded to the outcry from victims and victim advocates by mandating that kits in all alleged sexual assaults be DNA tested.

But what do we know, empirically, about the value of DNA testing large numbers of sexual assault kits (SAKs) that have long been held in police property rooms? And what do we know, empirically, about the crime-solving utility of testing kits in all alleged sexual assaults?

One thing we know is that the probative value of forensic evidence in any crime, including sexual assault,

depends largely on the circumstances of the case — pivotal in one, less important in another. If the perpetrator is a stranger to the victim, a DNA profile can be crucial in identifying the suspect and adjudicating the case. However, at least half of sexual assault victims know the perpetrator's identity; if he admits sexual contact but claims it was consensual, DNA evidence may be of questionable value in adjudicating the case — although it could have value in uncovering serial so-called "acquaintance" rapes. And, finally, when sexual assault is perpetrated on a child, DNA evidence is vital in determining that a crime occurred.

NIJ provided grant support to examine the role of DNA testing of untested SAKS in property

4

rooms of the Los Angeles Police Department (LAPD) and the Los Angeles Sheriff's Department (LASD). The grant was modest — $100,000 — and, therefore, the study had a narrow focus, including time limitations.

The two primary goals in the L.A. study were to look at a random sample of the nearly 11,000 kits to:

- Assess the efficacy of DNA testing

- Determine the criminal justice outcomes (arrest, charge, conviction) within the first six months after the kits were DNA tested

The findings with respect to the study's second goal were surprising to many. In a randomly selected sample of 371 SAKs, there were no new arrests, new charges were filed in one case, and there were two convictions in the first six months after these kits were tested. In fact, it is probable that the DNA testing was not responsible for the single filing and the two convictions.

There are a number of important facts to keep in mind when trying to understand these results. First, the study looked at case adjudication in only the first six months after testing, as this was the period defined in the NIJ grant. The researchers did not examine whether there have been additional arrests, charges filed or convictions since that time. Second, the sample size was small, and the findings are from one site; therefore, great caution should be used in trying to extend the findings to other locales. Indeed, the reasons for large numbers of untested SAKs in police property rooms — and the testing and case status of the kits themselves — may be very different in other jurisdictions.

> Recordkeeping that allows key criminal justice stakeholders to determine why a kit was not previously tested rarely exists, particularly in a searchable, electronic database.

One possible explanation for the findings is that a large number of the more than 10,000 SAKs in police storage had not been sent to the laboratory precisely *because* detectives and prosecutors had previously determined that testing would not increase the likelihood of adjudication. It was, however, beyond the scope of the NIJ study to analyze *why* the kits in L.A. city and county had not been tested, except anecdotally through focus groups with detectives, prosecutors and laboratory analysts.

That said, the L.A. study findings provide more empirical knowledge in an area in which there has been relatively little solid research to inform an important, controversial challenge facing our nation today: untested evidence in sexual assault cases and the role of DNA testing in solving these cases.

The L.A. Sexual Assault Kit Study

By fall 2008, there were 10,895 SAKs in the LAPD and LASD property rooms that had not been sent to a crime laboratory for analysis. (This is sometimes erroneously referred to

as a "backlog," but that term applies only to cases that *have* been submitted to a crime laboratory for analysis but have not yet been analyzed.) Although it was assumed that some of the SAKs were untested because investigators had concluded that testing was unwarranted — cases, for example, in which the perpetrator had been convicted or entered a guilty plea without DNA evidence, or cases in which investigators had concluded no crime occurred — it was unknown how many of these kits could yield probative DNA evidence, identify perpetrators and support successful adjudications if they were tested.

In 2009, Human Rights Watch, which had been looking at the issue of sexual assaults in L.A., reported that:[1]

- The county and city crime labs did not have the capacity to test all of the stored SAKs, let alone test new ones as they came in.

- It was taking up to a year from the time a request for DNA testing was made until a final laboratory report was completed.

- Victims were rarely informed of the status of their case.

L.A. officials made the decision to perform DNA testing on all of the nearly 11,000 SAKs in the LAPD and LASD property rooms. They found additional funding (including through NIJ's Backlog Reduction Grant Program) to outsource the testing to private labs.

This situation presented NIJ with a unique opportunity. All around the country, jurisdictions were realizing that large amounts of untested evidence in alleged sexual assault cases had not been sent to a laboratory for testing. The problem was that no one *knew* if there would be value — in terms of solving crimes and garnering justice for the victims and society — in testing them.

To help address this issue, NIJ funded researchers at California State University, Los Angeles, to look at two random samples. In the first, they looked at 1,948 cases to determine how successful testing would be in detecting a DNA profile that could be uploaded to the Combined DNA Index System (CODIS). The researchers also examined a second, smaller sample (371 cases from the first sample) to determine the impact DNA testing had on case adjudications in the first six months after kits were tested. Finally, the researchers conducted focus groups with LAPD and LASD detectives, prosecutors and lab analysts.

Testing Results and Case Characteristics

One of the primary goals of the study was to help answer these questions with respect to the untested SAKs in L.A.:

- What kind of evidence did the SAKs contain, and what would DNA testing reveal?

- How frequently was semen identified?

- How frequently was a male DNA profile obtained?

- How many profiles were uploaded to CODIS, and how many "hits" resulted? (For more on CODIS, see sidebar, "CODIS: The National DNA Database.")

Figure 1 (on p. 7) presents the findings of a randomly selected 20 percent sample (1,948 cases) in the L.A. study. The dark blue line at the top shows the total 1,948 cases that were studied. As the cases moved through DNA testing —

CODIS: The National DNA Database

The Combined DNA Index System (CODIS) is a database in which DNA profiles from crime scenes and convicted offenders (and, in some states, arrestees) are stored. CODIS — which includes local (LDIS), state (SDIS) and national (NDIS) databases — can be searched to determine if a DNA profile pulled from biological evidence in a crime matches the DNA of a known offender or DNA from evidence in another crime. These searches can generate leads for investigators when matches, or "hits," occur.

As of 2010, CODIS contained more than 8.7 million offender profiles and approximately 330,000 profiles from crime-scene evidence.

Searching CODIS can potentially have both immediate benefits (offering investigative leads in the current case) and long-term benefits (potentially linking an assailant to other crimes or linking cases together). Many states now collect DNA from all felony arrestees, which is greatly expanding CODIS and increasing the opportunity for hits. (For more information on arrestee DNA collection, see "Collecting DNA from Arrestees: Implementation Lessons," page 18.)

going from the top of the diagram to the bottom — some yielded results that could help investigators solve cases, and some did not. Obviously, one important "bottom line" of any CODIS hit is whether the hit provides a true investigatory lead that might help solve a case; the dark blue boxes at the bottom of the figure represent the cases in which DNA testing yielded investigative leads.

When the 1,948 SAKs were screened for DNA, DNA was present in 68 percent of the cases (1,320 cases, shown in light blue on the diagram's second line). DNA was not present, however, in 32 percent of the cases (628 cases, shown in gray on the second line), so the lab did not further test these.

The third line shows that "foreign" DNA — DNA from someone other than the alleged victim — was found in 81 percent of the cases in which there was DNA (shown in light blue). In 19 percent of the cases in which there was DNA, however, no foreign DNA was found (shown in gray).

Moving down the graph to the fourth line, 65 percent of the cases in which there was foreign DNA yielded profiles that were able to be uploaded into CODIS (699 cases, shown in blue). However, 35 percent of the cases in which there was foreign DNA did *not* yield a profile that was able to be uploaded into CODIS (371 cases, shown in gray).

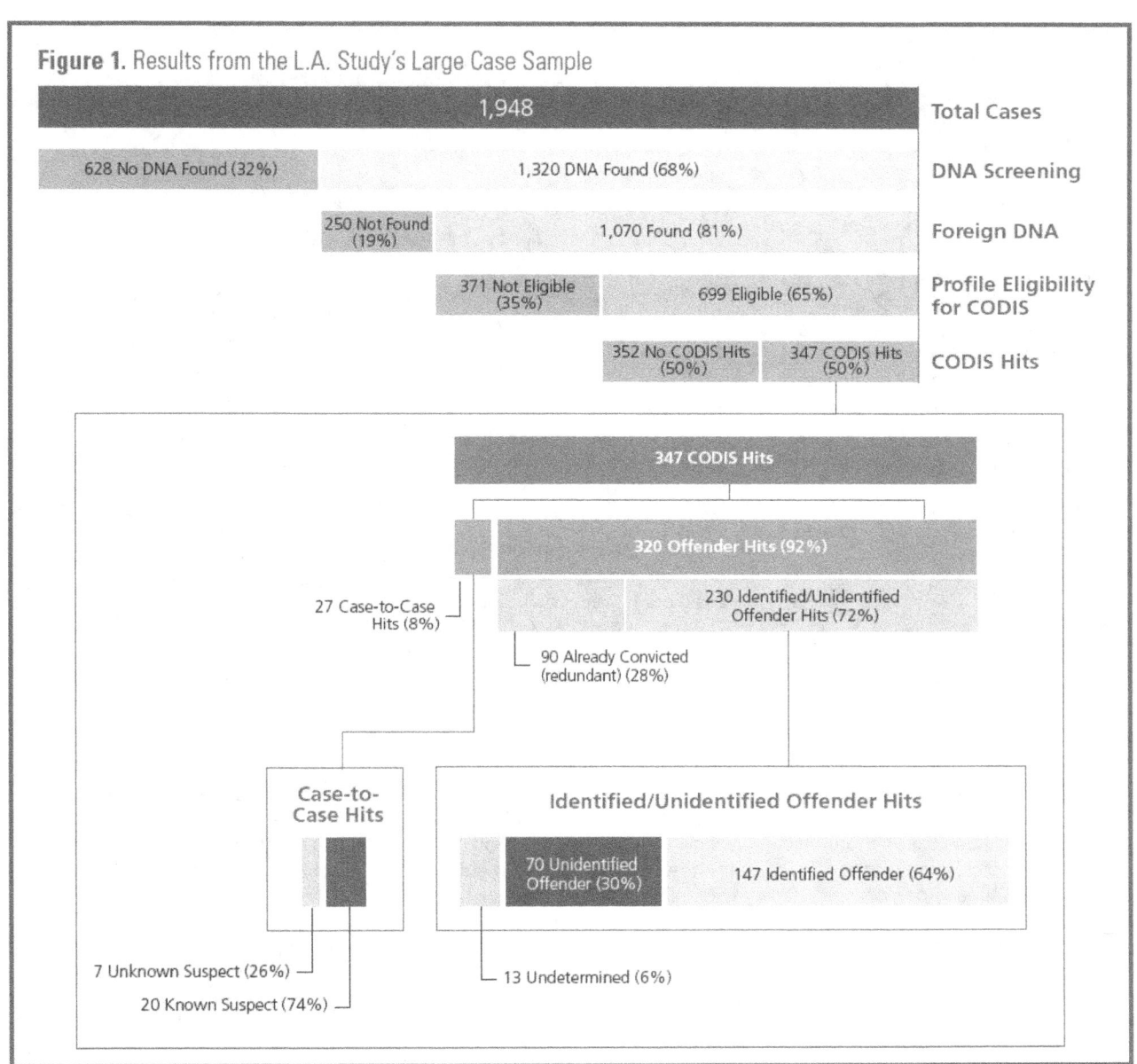

Figure 1. Results from the L.A. Study's Large Case Sample

Of the 699 cases that were uploaded into CODIS, about half resulted in hits (347 cases, blue segment), and about half did not (352 cases, gray segment). It is important to understand that even though there were hits in only half of the L.A. sample cases that were uploaded to CODIS, it is not known whether the profiles that did not result in hits may match future cases. (For more on this, see sidebar, "Case Characteristics of Untested Sexual Assault Kits in Los Angeles.")

There are two kinds of hits when a DNA profile matches a profile in CODIS: an "offender" hit and a "case-to-case" hit.

In the 347 cases in which there was a CODIS hit, 92 percent (320 cases) were "offender" hits (the right branch), and 8 percent (27 cases) were "case-to-case" hits (the left branch).

Offender Hits

Of the 320 offender hits, 28 percent (90 cases) merely re-identified the semen donor who had already been convicted of or had pled guilty to the very crime represented by

Case Characteristics of Untested Sexual Assault Kits in Los Angeles

One of the goals of the NIJ-funded study of sexual assault kits (SAKs) in the property rooms of the Los Angeles Police Department and the Los Angeles Sheriff's Department was to determine some of the case characteristics. The researchers did this by looking at a 20 percent random sample of the previously untested SAKs. Here are some of the findings:

- Ninety-four percent of the victims were female.

- Ninety-two percent of the assailants were male.

- The average age of the victims was 22 years; approximately 40 percent of the victims were under 18.

- Sixty-five percent of the victims knew the assailant.

- Seventy-seven percent of the victims reported vaginal penetration by the penis, a finger or a foreign object.

- Anal penetration was attempted or achieved in 32 percent of the cases.

- The assailant engaged in non-genital acts in 58 percent of the cases; the most common were kissing (39 percent), fondling (14 percent) and licking (14 percent).

- Twenty-nine percent of the victims reported that the assailant used contraceptives or lubricants; victims reported that the assailants used condoms in 11 percent of the assaults.

- Victims said they believed the assailant ejaculated in 28 percent of the cases.

- A great majority of the victims — 80 percent — engaged in some form of post-assault hygiene prior to the sexual-assault exam:

  • Seventy-three percent urinated or defecated.

  • Fifty-five percent ate, drank, gargled, rinsed or brushed their teeth.

  • Fifty-four percent used a genital wipe or douche.

  • Forty-six percent changed their clothing.

the kit — *without* the SAK having been tested. His DNA was entered into CODIS upon his conviction (or arrest), and this CODIS hit was to this same, previous case. Therefore, these hits, depicted in the gray segment as "already convicted (redundant)" on the diagram, did not yield any new information that could help in a particular investigation.

Of the 320 offender hits, 72 percent (230 cases) were to someone who had been arrested for or convicted of another crime. These hits can be to an identified offender (what law enforcement calls a "warm" hit) or to an unidentified offender (what law enforcement refers to as a "cold" hit). An *identified offender* hit is when the profile matches a named suspect, someone whose identity was already known or who was arrested in the case. DNA testing for an identified offender hit does not yield any additional investigative

information that law enforcement could follow up on, unless the suspect denies sexual contact. An *unidentified offender* hit occurs when the profile matches an arrestee or convicted offender whose identity was previously unknown — these, indeed, could yield new investigative information.

In the 230 offender hits in the L.A. study:

- Sixty-four percent (147 cases) were to identified offenders; that is, to people whose identity was known by the victim (light blue segment).

- Thirty percent (70 cases) were to unidentified offenders; that is, to people whose identity was unknown to the victim (dark blue segment).

- Six percent (13 cases) were to offenders whose relationship to

the victim could not be determined by the researchers; that is, the case file did not reveal whether the victim had known the identity of the suspect or not (gray segment).

NIJ is continuing to study the criminal-justice value of DNA testing, depending on whether the victim knows the identity of the alleged attacker, to learn whether this factor should be used as a testing prioritization criterion.

Case-to-Case Hits

The case-to-case hits in the L.A. study sample are depicted in the left branch of the diagram (at the very bottom). A case-to-case hit is when a newly tested SAK yields a DNA profile that matches a profile in another case in CODIS (which may or may not be a sexual assault). There were 27 case-to-case hits after the

1,948 SAKs in the L.A. study sample were DNA tested. Approximately three-fourths of these case-to-case hits (20 cases out of 27; dark blue segment on the diagram) linked to another case in which the suspect's identity was known. One-quarter of the case-to-case hits (seven cases; gray segment) linked to another case in which the suspect's identity was not known — that is, his DNA profile was known, but his name was not. Obviously, only known-suspect case-to-case hits provide an investigative lead for police to follow up on, but certainly "linking" unknown-suspect cases would become important if the profile is ever identified by name; a case-to-case hit also might help investigators establish the existence of a pattern, even if the alleged perpetrator's identity is not known.

In summary, then, after DNA testing an SAK, there are basically two types of CODIS hits that can generate a new investigative lead to help solve *that* case: a hit to a previously

unidentified offender (someone whose identity was not previously known to the victim) or a case-to-case hit to a case in which there is a known suspect.

Looking at the new investigatory leads — or the impact of DNA testing in the total sample of 1,948 previously untested SAKs in the L.A. study — DNA testing led to a suspect being identified in 90 cases: 70 in which there was an previously unidentified offender hit (4 percent of the total kits tested), and 20 in which there was a case-to-case known suspect hit (1 percent of the total kits tested). Note that it was beyond the scope of the study for the researchers to determine what happened to these leads.

Criminal Justice Outcomes

One of the goals of the L.A. study was to look at a smaller, randomly selected subset of the 1,948 cases — 371 cases — to determine

the number of new arrests, charges, convictions and sentences — called criminal-justice "outcomes" — that resulted within six months of testing.

As noted in the beginning of this article, there were no new arrests after these 371 kits were DNA tested. Although charges were filed in one new case, and there were two convictions (which includes the case in which charges were filed) after the SAKs were tested, it is doubtful that the testing was relevant to these case outcomes. In one conviction, sperm was detected on rectal and dried secretion samples, but DNA testing had not been done. In the other, Y-chromosome testing yielded the presence of male DNA, but no foreign DNA was found when the samples were subjected to short tandem repeat analysis. (For more on what the L.A. study showed with respect to DNA-testing methods, see sidebar, "DNA Testing: Techniques and Results in the Los Angeles Study.")

DNA Testing: Techniques and Results in the Los Angeles Study

DNA testing can be a powerful tool in identifying or excluding suspects in sexual assaults. A suspect's DNA profile can be obtained from semen and cells left on the victim. Dried semen, saliva or other body secretions on bedding, clothing or towels can also yield a DNA profile, as can cells left on the exterior or interior of a discarded condom.

The NIJ-funded study of untested sexual assault evidence in L.A. found that:

- Y-chromosome testing (to determine the presence of male DNA) and conventional

serology screening techniques (including microscopic examination to determine the presence of sperm cells) had comparable success rates in leading to positive short tandem repeat results. However, the Y-chromosome technique was more successful in detecting foreign and male DNA in samples taken from the vaginal and external genitalia areas and dried secretions.

- In developing full and partial profiles, the Y-chromosome screening technique was superior with samples from external genitalia, and conventional serology techniques were more successful with

samples from the rectal area. Success was mixed in samples taken from the oral and vaginal areas and from dried secretions.

It should be noted that screening evidence for presence of the Y-chromosome does not yield a male DNA profile; that is, it does not identify the suspect. Also, Y-chromosome screening does not distinguish the tissue type, so the Y chromosome could have come from epithelial cells in saliva, or from semen, blood or skin cells; this type of information could affect the way a crime is eventually charged.

NIJ's Action-Research Project in Houston and Detroit

In April 2011, NIJ awarded competitive research grants to Wayne County (Detroit) and Houston to examine the issue of untested evidence in sexual assaults. At that time, it was believed that there were more than 16,000 untested sexual assault kits (SAKs) in the Houston Police Department property room and more than 10,000 in Detroit police custody.

The NIJ-funded teams in Houston and Detroit include criminal justice researchers; sexual assault forensic examiners; and representatives from the police department, crime lab and community-based victim services organizations. One of the primary goals of the "action research" project is to produce transportable lessons and strategies to help other jurisdictions that have untested SAKs in their property rooms.

"Action research" is a method in which researchers engage in an active partnership with practitioner agencies to solve a problem. As former NIJ program manager Lois Mock and her co-authors explain in a 2010 article, the researchers play a key role in identifying the problem and analyzing the data and in working with the practitioner agency to develop intervention strategies to target the problem.[1] The practitioner agency implements the strategies, and the researchers monitor progress and provide feedback to better refine the strategies. Finally, the researchers conduct an assessment of the implementation of the problem-solving strategies and their impacts.

The Houston and Detroit projects were broken into two phases. The first was a six-month planning phase. The teams are now into the second, implementation, phase. Although it is too early to report any definite findings, some interesting preliminary data have emerged.

One of the Detroit team's goals in phase 1 was to get an accurate count of how many SAKs in police custody were, in fact, untested. Their audit has determined that, as of November 1, 2009, there were 8,505 untested SAKs in police storage.

A second goal in Detroit was to examine why the problem developed in the first place. Based on an analysis of 20 years of archival records (public records and internal records) and on in-depth interviews with key stakeholders from all multidisciplinary groups, researchers Rebecca Campbell and Giannina Fehler-Cabral from Michigan State University have identified reasons why there were so many untested SAKs in Detroit. In essence, they say, the following can be regarded as "risk factors" for a large number of untested SAKs:

- Lack of a formal policy and protocol for kit testing

- Reduction in staffing levels within law enforcement due to budget cuts, which can significantly curtail sexual assault investigations

- Very high turnover in law enforcement leadership and supervision of the sex crimes unit

- Reduction in staffing levels in the crime lab due to budget cuts

- Use of inefficient DNA testing equipment/methodology within the crime lab due to budget cuts

It is important to understand that, when officials made the decision to test all previously untested kits stored in the LAPD and LASD property rooms, there was no attempt to weed out cases that had previously been adjudicated (that is, adjudicated *without* the benefit of the SAK being tested). The researchers found that, in the random sample of 371 cases, a suspect had been arrested in nearly 40 percent of the cases (147 arrests) without the benefit of DNA analysis.

Charges had been filed in 81 of the 371 sample cases, and 65 cases (nearly 18 percent of the sample) had ended in a conviction.

This confirms one thing that we already know: In many cases, DNA testing of evidence is not necessary for there to be a plea or conviction in a sexual assault case. Based on the results in the L.A. study, the researchers found, in fact, that there was little *immediate* criminal-justice value in testing the large number of previously untested SAKs that were in the LAPD and LASD property rooms. What is unknown, of course, is whether there may be future dividends — that is, the potential to solve future crimes — from uploading the profiles to CODIS in cases that had not been previously adjudicated.

NIJ is currently involved in research projects in Houston and Detroit

- Lack of good-quality sexual assault medical forensic exams

- Lack of community-based sexual assault advocacy services

- Lack of professional training for all multidisciplinary service providers

Currently, Detroit is testing a sample of the previously untested SAKs and developing victim-notification protocols.

In Houston, one of the most significant early findings concerns the number of untested kits. As part of its preparation for moving to a new evidence-storage facility, the Houston Police Department performed an audit of all SAKs in its custody. As a result of the audit, officials have determined that there are far fewer untested SAKs in Houston than previously believed. The NIJ project is focusing on approximately 4,000 kits that have been stored in the freezer, of which about one-third (1,200 kits) have been screened by the lab in the past couple of years.

In the first phase of the project, Noel Busch-Armendariz, Director of the Institute on Domestic Violence and Sexual Assault at the University of Texas at Austin, and her team — along with William Wells from Sam Houston State University, co-principal investigator on the NIJ project — conducted 146 interviews of law enforcement investigators, prosecutors, laboratory analysts, sexual assault nurse examiners, victim advocates and victims. The interviews are helping the team develop an in-depth understanding of untested sexual assault evidence in Houston.

Final results from the Houston and Detroit projects are expected in 2014.

Note

1. Mock, Lois Felson, "Action Research for Crime Control and Prevention," in *New Criminal Justice: American Communities and the Changing World of Crime Control*, ed. John Klofas, Natalie Kroovand Hipple and Edmund McGarrel. New York: Routledge, 2010: 97-102.

and criminalists from the LAPD and LASD. Such qualitative information can help frame and give greater context to quantitative data, and this can be especially important when other scientific evidence is still being developed to inform policy and practice. The L.A. focus groups looked particularly at the role SAK evidence plays in resolving stranger and non-stranger sexual assaults.

Perhaps the most commonly expressed sentiment among the participants was that mandatory testing of kits was unnecessary when the suspect's identity was already known, and the legal issue was consent. Noting that laboratory resources are limited, participants stated that a system of priorities should be established to determine which SAKs — and what specific evidence within the kits — would have probative value. (For more, see sidebar, "The Los Angeles Focus Groups.")

Why Are SAKs Not Sent to Laboratories for Testing?

The reasons that large numbers of SAKs are stored in police property rooms around the country are complex. As mentioned previously, kits that have not been sent to a crime lab are not technically part of what is often referred to as the "backlog," because investigators or prosecutors have not submitted them to a laboratory and requested that they be analyzed. Within the criminal justice community, the term "backlog" applies to cases that have been waiting for testing in a crime lab for more than 30 days. In fact, it is problematic to regard all untested SAKs in police property rooms as part of a crime laboratory backlog. Doing so oversimplifies — and could even obscure — the reasons that SAKs are not sent to a crime lab for analysis.

where the jurisdictions are first determining if kits stored in their property rooms have already been tested or the cases have already been adjudicated before coming up with a plan to do DNA testing. (For more on this, see sidebar, "NIJ's Action-Research Project in Houston and Detroit.")

NIJ is also building on the L.A. study results through a recently funded project in Massachusetts. This work is intended to add to our body of knowledge about when DNA testing may — and may not — be necessary to move a case forward. (For more on that project, see sidebar, "Understanding DNA Testing in Sexual Assaults: NIJ's Ongoing Work in Massachusetts.")

Input From Focus Groups

In the L.A. study, the researchers held focus groups with sexual assault investigators, prosecuting attorneys

Understanding DNA Testing in Sexual Assaults: NIJ's Ongoing Work in Massachusetts

Last year, NIJ awarded $97,000 to the University of Illinois to study the role of forensic evidence in the criminal justice outcomes of sexual assault cases. Researchers are looking at a random sample of 436 sexual assaults that occurred in 2008-2010 in Massachusetts. The goals of the study are to:

▪ Provide a detailed description of forensic evidence to determine the frequency of different types of evidence

▪ Assess the timing of when forensic evidence is available with respect to arrests and charges filed

▪ Examine the relationship among forensic evidence, arrests and charging

▪ Analyze the role of forensic evidence, particularly in cases with child victims and cases in which the perpetrator is a stranger

▪ Compare the impact of sexual assault nurse examiners (SANEs) versus non-SANE evidence collectors on arrests and charges filed

The researchers will use a variety of methods (including descriptive and bivariate statistics and logistic regression analyses) to analyze data from three sources: mandatory reports by medical providers collected in the state Executive Office of Public Safety and Security database, non-electronic crime lab data, and police incident data from the National Incident-Based Reporting System and a Boston Police Department database.

Findings from the study are expected in 2013.

That said, it is crucial that jurisdictions determine which SAKs stored in their property rooms have previously been DNA tested and which have not but could have probative value if tested. In Houston, for example, where an NIJ-funded project is looking at the issue of untested evidence in sexual assault cases, authorities have determined that approximately half of the stored SAKs had previously been screened by the crime lab (see sidebar, "NIJ's Action-Research Project in Houston and Detroit"). This raises the question of whether a large percentage of SAKs in the property rooms of some jurisdictions may have already been tested.

Regardless of what future research tells us about the percentage of stored SAKs that have already been tested, it is clear that many SAKs have *not* been tested. To gather more data about this issue, NIJ commissioned a nationwide survey a few years ago to try to understand why forensic evidence in a variety of crimes, including sexual assault, was not being sent to a crime lab for analysis. More than 2,000 state and local law enforcement departments responded.

The findings, published in 2009, revealed that forensic evidence — including DNA, fingerprints, firearms and tool marks — was not submitted to a crime lab in 18 percent of unsolved sexual assaults, 14 percent of unsolved homicides and 23 percent of unsolved property crimes during 2002-2007.[2]

Of course, there are legitimate reasons why law enforcement might not send forensic evidence to a lab, including a belief that it would not be probative, or knowledge that the charges have been dropped or that a guilty plea has already been entered in the case. However, the RTI International researchers who performed the survey concluded that some law enforcement officers might not fully understand the value of forensic evidence in developing new investigatory leads. Here are some of the findings:

Reason evidence not sent to the laboratory	Percentage of agencies citing as a reason
No suspect had been identified	44%
Uncertain of its usefulness	30%
Suspect adjudicated without testing	24%
Case dismissed	19%
Prosecutor did not request testing	15%

DNA-Testing Decisions

Perhaps the most frequent reason that an SAK is not sent to a lab for DNA testing is that the victim knows the identity of the assailant: He is a domestic or intimate partner; he is a family member or they are dating; or they have a work-related or casual relationship. In these cases, if the suspect admits sexual contact, but maintains that it was consensual, authorities (in jurisdictions without a "test-all" policy) are unlikely to think that DNA testing would be probative. Although the percentage of these "known-suspect" cases varies from jurisdiction to jurisdiction, studies have shown that 48-75 percent of sexual assault victims know the identity of the assailant.[3-7]

One of the goals of the L.A. study was to determine *why* investigators or prosecutors had not requested DNA analysis when the SAKs were first collected. This presented an insurmountable, if not altogether surprising, hurdle.

One of the greatest challenges authorities faced when confronting the nearly 11,000 SAKs in the LAPD and LASD property rooms — and which other jurisdictions around the country now face — was determining *why* an SAK was not tested at the time of the alleged crime. In fact, the LASD performed an audit of its untested SAKs and determined that many of the cases had been adjudicated without the kits' being DNA tested. But, put simply, recordkeeping that allows key criminal justice stakeholders to determine why a kit was not previously tested rarely exists, particularly in a searchable, electronic database. And without easily searchable records, it can be very difficult to determine if the detective decided not to send a kit to the lab because the alleged perpetrator's identity was already known and DNA testing may not have been a wise use of resources, or if the kit should have been tested, and testing it now could potentially solve the case.

Neither the LAPD nor LASD has a computer system that tracks sexual assault evidence and key decisions made along the way. Looking again at the 2009 RTI survey of 2,000 police departments, this finding was significant: Only 43 percent of the departments said they had a computerized system that allowed them to track information about evidence in a case. That statistic was even lower for mid-size and small departments. And, of course, the existence of a

> It is crucial that jurisdictions determine which SAKs stored in their property rooms have previously been DNA tested, and which have not but could have probative value if tested.

computerized system that *connects* law enforcement, the lab and the prosecutor's office is rarer still.

Take this example: If a detective working a sexual assault case in 1990 did not *document* his decision in a database, case file or evidence log that the SAK was not being sent to the lab for DNA analysis because the suspect was known to the victim and the legal issue was "consent" — or if the suspect had pled or been found guilty — it is very difficult to know now whether testing that SAK *now* would help solve the case.

In the L.A. study, the researchers found that information on the decision to test — or not test — an SAK was not consistently documented. Pertinent data may or may not have existed in the police incident report, the sexual assault exam report, the victim's statement, the arrest report or the prosecutor's file. Unfortunately, resources did not allow the researchers to try to track down this information.

Determining the status of an SAK in police storage — Has it been tested? Is the suspect's identity already known because the victim knew him? Was the case adjudicated? — is vexingly difficult to do in many jurisdictions. In Houston, for example, where NIJ is currently studying the issue, authorities have devoted significant time and human resources to "auditing" the SAKs in the police property room to determine their testing and case-outcome status.

Ultimately, what this means is that, unless a jurisdiction has the resources to test every SAK in its custody — at a minimum of $1,000 per kit — determining details about a kit that allow authorities to triage testing is labor-intensive and expensive. In this regard, it is also important to note that many people support a policy of testing *all* stored SAKs and all evidence in new sexual assault cases. (For more information, see sidebar, "The Case for Testing All Sexual Assault Kits.")

Applying Lessons Learned

Public resources are finite. We are in a period of cutbacks at every level of government. At the same time, sexual assault victims and the public are demanding justice in unsolved sexual assaults.

In the end, it is science that can help practitioners and policymakers make the most efficacious and fiscally responsible decisions on how best to solve sexual assault cases. The

The Los Angeles Focus Groups

One of the goals of the Los Angeles sexual assault kit (SAK) study was to talk to boots-on-the-ground practitioners. Lead researcher Joe Peterson and his California State University team held four focus groups. Here are some of the main points made in the focus groups.

Law enforcement investigators

Although most of the detectives said that they had not yet found the Combined DNA Index System (CODIS) valuable in linking sexual assault cases, they cited the "Grim Sleeper" serial murders as a recent example of how DNA testing could link a decades-old case to a single offender. The detectives said that as the CODIS database grows, it will become a more useful investigative tool.

The detectives expressed no doubt that DNA testing in sexual assault cases can be valuable; however, they questioned the need to test all SAKs. Some said they believed that the recently adopted policy of testing all kits was an overreaction, saying that it removed their discretion. Some questioned the wisdom of testing all SAKs when time and human resources are limited, especially in cases that are unlikely to result in prosecution. They also noted that the current test-all policy results in some testing delays and, ultimately, amounts to poor case management when caseloads are already heavy.

The detectives discussed the importance of communicating with lab analysts. They noted that the SAK testing request form allows them to direct the lab to specific pieces of evidence within the kit that, based on the history provided by the victim, could most likely yield a DNA profile. However, some detectives conceded that, although the lab request form does not preclude additional communication with analysts, they did not always speak with the analysts or only followed up on some cases.

The detectives also mentioned occasional difficulty understanding scientific terminology in lab reports and that better communication with the analyst would help them better comprehend the results. They noted the importance of maintaining awareness of scientific results and database inquiries and coordinating the sharing of information with victims.

Deputy district attorneys

The deputy district attorneys' belief mirrored the detectives' belief that DNA testing of an SAK has tremendous corroborative value in meeting legal standards of evidence and supporting the victim's credibility. However, some prosecutors felt that the length of time and cost of testing were prohibitive, and most said that testing is not strictly necessary if there is other corroborative evidence, such as a suspect's admission or a victim's injuries. Note, however, that this does not address the possible value of using CODIS to link the suspect to other past or future crimes.

They characterized the decision to test an SAK as "fact-driven," based on each case, adding that even though corroboration of victim statements and victim credibility are key criteria in deciding whether to charge a suspect, it is not mandatory to have DNA results in every case. The prosecutors agreed with the detectives that testing is probably not necessary if the suspect's identity is not in question or if "consent" is the issue

L.A. study — although only one study of one city and county's experiences — offers another piece of the puzzle. Most significantly, the study — and, in fact, NIJ's growing body of knowledge in sexual assault and the use of forensic evidence — points to this reality: The nation's criminal justice agencies need computerized databases that link crucial data — including documented decision-making — from police investigation files, the sexual assault exam, lab testing of the SAK and the prosecutor's office. Such databases also would allow an objective review, by police oversight boards, for example, to provide better transparency about decision-making processes and the quality of investigative and forensic services.

Indeed, this issue is at the heart of recommendations made by the L.A. study researchers. Going forward, they said, jurisdictions should form an SAK advisory committee with representatives from law enforcement, the crime lab and the forensic medical community to:

■ Develop criteria for submitting SAKs to the lab and criteria for deciding which kits should be DNA tested.

when both individuals are underage; however, they strongly supported testing when it is key to establishing that a crime occurred or could possibly identify the suspect.

Some prosecutors said that policies mandating the testing of all SAKs were being driven by community perceptions, including that the public generally regards *not* testing evidence in an alleged sexual assault as violating the victim's rights. Such expectations, they said, have been compounded by TV shows that do not foster a full understanding of DNA testing. 'Juries expect it,' they said. 'They're going to wonder why when the kit isn't tested.' The prosecutors noted that, when an SAK is not tested, they must offer an explanation during *voir dire* or trial. It is vital, they added, to educate potential jurors on 'what science can and cannot do' because of expectations formed by *CSI*-type dramas.

Some of the prosecutors suggested that lab delays were sometimes caused by detectives requesting that the lab test everything. The researchers reported that this seemed contrary to the detectives' belief in their ability to direct the testing of

evidence and seemed to suggest that the prosecutors did not believe that detectives always knew what particular evidence within an SAK would be most useful to a case.

The prosecutors said that lab analysts appreciated when they (the prosecutors) were knowledgeable about different types of DNA analysis and the associated costs, particularly in light of the presence or absence of other evidence in a case.

Finally, the prosecutors agreed with the detectives that labs should establish testing priorities to determine which kits should be tested and which evidence within an SAK should be tested.

Laboratory analysts

The lab analysts generally felt that their mission — to help solve cases — was being complicated by their parent agencies' new policy to test all SAKs. They regarded this as turning the lab's mission into uploading profiles into CODIS, regardless of whether the suspect's profile in the case was already in CODIS. Although they acknowledged the long-term benefits that could be gained from increasing the size of the CODIS

database, they said that many of the hits resulting from testing all SAKs in the property rooms were for defendants who had already been convicted. They also said that, to their knowledge, none of the hits had led to a defendant being exonerated.

The analysts told the researchers that, if the detectives felt that testing all SAKs eliminated their discretion, they felt this even more strongly. "We don't get to triage; we get told what to do," one said. "We just do what comes in the door," said another. The lab analysts agreed with the detectives and prosecutors that some cases were being tested unnecessarily, noting that lab resources could be used more efficiently, specifically in stranger sexual assaults.

The analysts noted difficulty staying current with workload, saying that although new analysts were being hired, it was difficult to train them quickly to begin working on cases. They said that the response to the untested SAKs in L.A. seemed more like crisis management, adding that strategic planning was necessary to come up with long-term solutions.

■ Establish mandatory data elements to be recorded, including why a decision was made not to send an SAK to the crime lab for testing.

The researchers also recommend that jurisdictions not start testing all SAKs in their custody until they know if the kit has been previously tested and whether the case has been adjudicated without being DNA

tested. Based on the L.A. study, for example, we see very clear evidence that unless authorities are able to determine if a kit has been tested before, they would (if the kits were tested now) not be able to determine if a CODIS hit occurs because the profile was previously put into CODIS from *that same case,* or if the hit is truly a new hit (cold hit) that could help investigators solve that case or other cases.

These are issues that the NIJ-funded teams in Detroit and Houston are further exploring.

"The bottom line," said Joe Peterson, lead researcher in the L.A. study, "is that we will never understand the value of forensic DNA testing in sexual assault until there are better data — consolidated in a single database

The Case for Testing All Sexual Assault Kits

There is significant support — particularly among victim advocates, policymakers, prosecutors and sexual assault survivors — for testing all sexual assault kits (SAKs). This includes the thousands of SAKs maintained in police property rooms as well as kits in every new sexual assault that occurs. Proponents of mandatory testing argue that testing SAKS even in non-stranger cases (48-75 percent of sexual assaults[3-7]) can potentially lead to the identification of a serial rapist, affirm the victim's version of events, discredit the assailant or exonerate an innocent suspect.

Advancements in DNA technology now allow smaller and more degraded pieces of biological evidence to be analyzed. Therefore, current DNA technologies can be used to solve cold cases and exonerate wrongly convicted people.

It is also possible to use DNA-testing results from cases that are not going to be adjudicated — if the statute of limitations has run, for example — in other ways. Testing results from an unadjudicated case may be deemed relevant in the parole hearing of a convicted offender, for example. It is also possible for a judge to allow evidence of past criminal behavior — even criminal behavior that was unadjudicated, if the court deems that it is directly relevant to the case at hand — under Federal Rule of Evidence 404(b).

Often referred to simply as "404(b)," this rule allows evidence regarding a defendant's character or prior criminal conduct into a trial under certain circumstances. Some proponents of analyzing all older SAKs argue that even if the statute of limitations has run, it could be important to have 404(b) evidence of a past sexual assault if the person is on trial in the future for another sexual assault. Especially in cases when the victim and the suspect know each other, the ability to present 404(b) evidence can effectively turn a "he-said, she-said" case into a case of "he-said, she-said, she-said."

> In the end, it is science that can help practitioners and policymakers make the most efficacious and fiscally responsible decisions on how best to solve sexual assault cases.

or in linked databases — maintained by all the agencies in the criminal justice system that are responsible for investigating and prosecuting sexual assaults."

This, Peterson said, is perhaps the most important recommendation coming out of the L.A. study: Better data management systems must be created to ensure that detectives, crime lab analysts and prosecutors have access to the most relevant information in a case.

"This kind of information," he added, "needs to be at the *fingertips* of criminal justice and crime lab professionals … not weeks, months or even years later."

About the author: Nancy Ritter is a writer and editor at NIJ.

NCJ 238483

For more information:

- Read the final report to the National Institute of Justice, *Sexual Assault Kit Backlog Study*, at https://www.ncjrs. gov/pdffiles1/nij/grants/238500.pdf.

- Read the NIJ Special Report, *The Road Ahead: Unanalyzed Evidence in Sexual Assault Cases*, at https://www. ncjrs.gov/pdffiles1/nij/233279.pdf.

- Read the NIJ Special Report, *Making Sense of DNA Backlogs: Myths vs. Reality*, at https://www.ncjrs.gov/ pdffiles1/nij/232197.pdf.

Check out NIJ's Web page on the action-research projects in Detroit and Houston: http://www.nij.gov/topics/forensics/sexual-assault-kits.htm.

Listen to researchers and practitioners in Los Angeles discuss how collaboration can improve the quality of sexual assault investigations and watch their presentations: http://www.nij.gov/multimedia/presenter/presenter-nijconf2011-collaboration.

Listen to a panel discussion on forensic information data exchange and the partnership between law enforcement and crime laboratories from the 2010 NIJ Conference: http://nij.ncjrs.gov/multimedia/audio-nijconf2010-data-exchange.htm.

Watch Rebecca Campbell's presentation on the impact of sexual assault nurse examiner programs on adult sexual assault investigation and prosecution: http://nij.ncjrs.gov/multimedia/video-sane.htm.

Notes

1. Human Rights Watch, *Testing Justice: The Rape Kit Backlog in Los Angeles City and County,* New York: Human Rights Watch, 2009: 1-61, available at http://www.hrw.org/sites/default/files/reports/rapekit0309web.pdf.

2. Strom, Kevin J., Jeri Ropero-Miller, Shelton Jones, Nathan Sikes, Mark Pope, and Nicole Hortsmann, "The 2007 Survey of Law Enforcement Evidence Processing," Final report to the National Institute of Justice, grant number 2007F 07165, October 2009, NCJ 228415, available at http://www.ncjrs.gov/pdffiles1/nij/grants/228415.pdf. See also Ritter, Nancy, "Untested Evidence: Not Just a Crime Lab Issue," *NIJ Journal,* 266 (2010): 28-30, available at http://www.nij.gov/journals/266/untested.htm.

3. Jänisch, Stefanie, Hildrun Meyer, Tanja Germerott, Urs-Vito Albrecht, Yvonne Schuz, and Anette Debertin Solveig, "Analysis of Clinical Forensic Examination Reports on Sexual Assault," *International Journal of Legal Medicine,* 124, 2010: 227-235.

4. Ingemann-Hansen, Ole, Ole Brink, Svend Sabroe, Villy Sørensen, and Annie Vesterbye Charles, "Legal Aspects of Sexual Violence — Does Forensic Evidence Make a Difference?" *Forensic Science International,* 180, 2008: 98-104.

5. Campbell, Rebecca, Debra Patterson, Deborah Bybee, and Emily R. Dworkin, "Predicting Sexual Assault Prosecution Outcomes: The Role of Medical Forensic Evidence Collected by Sexual Assault Nurse Examiners," *Criminal Justice and Behavior,* 36, 2009: 712-727.

6. McLean, Iain, Stephen A. Roberts, Cath White, and Sheila Paul, "Female Genital Injuries Resulting From Consensual and Non-Consensual Vaginal Intercourse," *Forensic Science International,* 240, 2011: 27-33.

7. Spohn, Cassia, Dawn Beichner, and Erika Davis-Frenzel, "Prosecutorial Justifications for Sexual Assault Case Rejection: Guarding the 'Gateway to Justice,'" *Social Problems,* 48, 2001: 206-235.

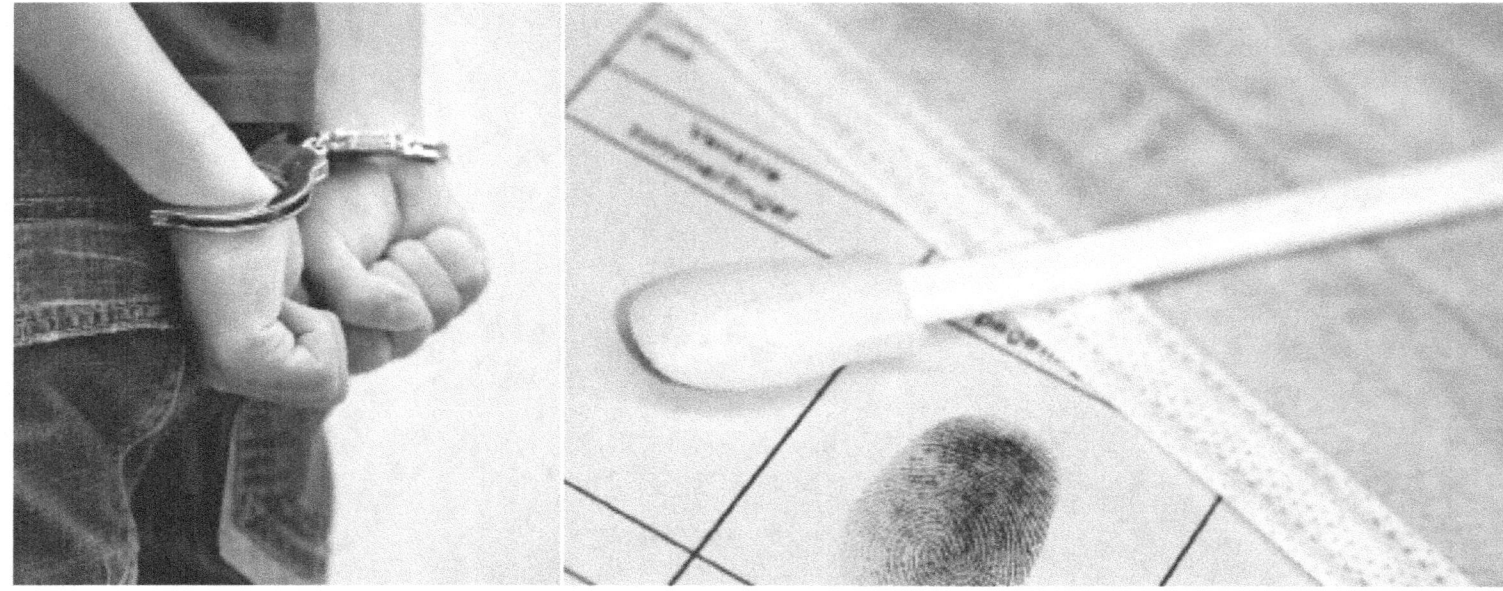

Collecting DNA From Arrestees:
Implementation Lessons

by Julie Samuels, Elizabeth Davies, Dwight Pope and Ashleigh Holand

Interim data from an Urban Institute study provide a detailed look at state arrestee DNA collection laws.

In the summer of 2011, a man was arrested for the abduction of a 15-year-old girl in the small Dayton, Ohio, suburb of Englewood.[1] A new state law, which expanded the pool of individuals eligible to have their DNA collected to include those arrested for a felony offense, allowed sheriff's deputies to collect a DNA sample from the arrested man. The sample was analyzed, and the resulting profile was entered into the Combined DNA Index System (CODIS), where it matched (or "hit") against a profile from forensic evidence collected in a rape committed a decade earlier. The man has been charged in both cases.

Similar stories of investigations aided by hits to arrestee DNA profiles[2] — along with cautionary tales of what can happen when a state fails to collect DNA in time[3] — have bolstered the arguments for collecting DNA samples not just from convicted offenders, but also from individuals arrested or charged with certain qualifying offenses. Twenty-eight states and the federal government have enacted laws that authorize such collection. Yet despite their widespread adoption, little is known about the investigative utility of collecting DNA from arrestees or how expanded DNA collection laws affect the collecting agencies and state crime laboratories responsible for their implementation.

This article explores the latter issue — how key provisions in arrestee DNA legislation influence the activities associated

with DNA collection and analysis. Information in this article was derived from a review of state and federal laws and from interviews with state crime laboratory representatives in 26 of the 28 states that passed legislation authorizing collection of DNA from some subset of arrestees.[4] This data collection is part of an NIJ-funded Urban Institute project examining the collection of DNA from arrestees.

A Growing Trend

The first state to pass legislation authorizing the collection of DNA samples from arrestees was Louisiana in 1997. The legislation authorized DNA sample collection from "a person arrested for a felony sex offense or other specified offense on or after September 1, 1999."[5] In the eight years that followed, four additional states passed arrestee DNA laws. The pace of expansion increased dramatically after Congress passed the DNA Fingerprint Act of 2005,[6] which, among other things, enabled states to upload arrestee DNA profiles to the National DNA Index System (NDIS). Between 2006 and 2011, 23 states passed arrestee DNA collection legislation. Today, 28 states and the federal government have passed legislation authorizing the collection of DNA following arrest or charging (see Figure 1). (To learn more about DNA databases, see sidebar, "CODIS: The National DNA Database" on page 6, in "Solving Sexual Assaults: Finding Answers Through Research.")

Supporters of these laws maintain that expanding DNA databases to include DNA profiles from arrestees will provide law enforcement with an additional tool to identify suspects, particularly those in unsolved cases, and potentially prevent future crimes. They note that even if a profile will

Studying the Implications of Expanding DNA Databases

In 2010, the Urban Institute began an NIJ-funded study to examine the policies, practices and implications of expanding state and federal DNA databases to include arrestees. Key research questions for the project include:

- How do the laws and policies regarding arrestee DNA collection differ by state?
- How have the laws been implemented in each state?
- What have been the challenges of requiring DNA collection from arrestees across the criminal justice system?
- What evidence is available regarding the effects of collecting DNA from arrestees on public safety or other justice outcomes?

To answer these questions, researchers have been reviewing and cataloging state laws, interviewing laboratory and criminal justice representatives in jurisdictions with arrestee DNA laws, and collecting descriptive statistics from states on the volume of arrestee profiles entered into the Combined DNA Index System and resulting hits. The final report, expected in late 2012, will explore issues identified in this article in greater detail, address broader issues concerning the rationale and benefits of arrestee DNA collection, and present findings from data collection and analysis.

ultimately be expunged (see "Who is responsible for initiating expungement?" on page 23), investigations may still benefit from the period of time prior to disposition when the arrestee DNA profile can be linked to DNA evidence collected from an unsolved criminal investigation and lead to the identification of a suspect in the "hit case."[7] Proponents argue that were it not for such laws, some individuals who are arrested but never convicted could "slip through the fingers of law enforcement"[8] and never have their DNA linked to additional crimes that they may have committed.

Others argue that the anticipated benefits do not justify the collection of DNA samples from citizens

who have not been convicted of the charges for which they were arrested. The constitutionality of collecting DNA from arrestees has been challenged as a violation of the Fourth Amendment's protection against unreasonable search and seizure in state and federal courts across the country. At this time, courts are split, with some upholding the expanded laws and others ruling them unconstitutional. Ultimately, the U.S. Supreme Court may be called upon to resolve the issue.[9]

Key Logistical Questions About Arrestee DNA Collection

State legislators have drafted their laws against this backdrop of competing perspectives on the benefits

Figure 1. States That Have Enacted Arrestee DNA Collection Laws in the United States

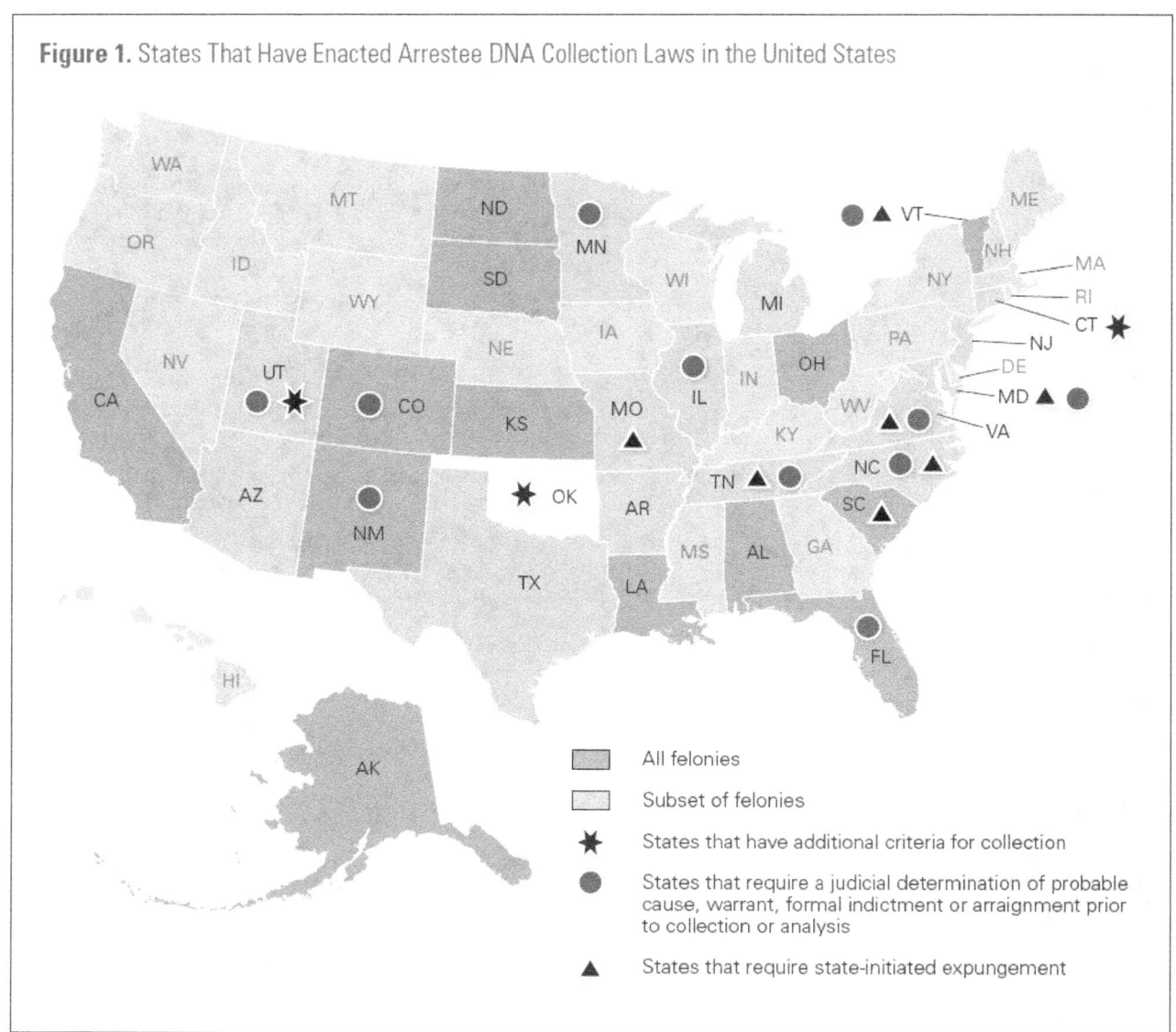

All felonies

Subset of felonies

★ States that have additional criteria for collection

● States that require a judicial determination of probable cause, warrant, formal indictment or arraignment prior to collection or analysis

▲ States that require state-initiated expungement

of arrestee DNA collection and the potential for legal challenges. Among the questions that legislators have addressed are:

▪ Which offenses are eligible for collection?

▪ At what point in criminal case processing can a sample be collected or analyzed?

▪ Who is responsible for collection?

▪ What policies govern the collection and analysis of duplicate samples?

▪ Who is responsible for initiating expungement?

The answers to these questions vary by state and have the potential to increase the workload and implementation burdens placed on

collecting agencies and the state crime laboratories responsible for analysis. In some instances, increased workloads will require additional staffing, technology, training and funding.

Which offenses are eligible for collection?

Our review of laws in the 28 states that passed legislation authorizing the collection of DNA samples prior to conviction reveals that about half of states (13) collect from all persons arrested for any felony crime, while the other half of states limit collection to a subset of felonies that typically involve violence or sexual assault.[10] Seven states also collect from individuals arrested or charged with select misdemeanor crimes.[11] Oklahoma, Connecticut and Utah have additional criteria for collection based on the arrestee's status, criminal history and health (respectively).

How does the decision to limit or expand the number of offenses that trigger collection affect the workload of collecting agencies and state crime laboratories? State laws that adopt broader eligibility criteria increase the number and variety of known profiles that may result in a match; hence, it makes sense to assume that as qualifying offenses increase, so too will the number of people sampled and the number of DNA samples processed. The total number of samples received is likely to decrease *eventually* as DNA samples collected at arrest supplant those that would have been collected following conviction;[12] however, our research suggests that limited laboratory staff, resources and space can restrict laboratories' ability to respond to the initial increase in sample volume, often resulting in the need for new staff, technological upgrades and larger facilities.

Some states have been able to mitigate the effect of new samples on laboratory staff workload by phasing in implementation over the course of several months or even years. For example, Florida passed legislation whereby the scope of qualifying offenses becomes more inclusive every two years until all felony

arrests are eligible for DNA collection; each phase is contingent upon the availability of state funds to support expanding laboratory activities.

Ironically, limiting the scope of collection to a subset of felony arrests may actually increase the administrative burden. Although there are fewer individuals for whom DNA must be collected and analyzed than in all-felon states, laboratory staff often must expend additional resources

> More than half of the states in this country currently authorize the collection of DNA from individuals who have been arrested or charged with a qualifying offense.

verifying offense eligibility, which can be particularly time-consuming. Collecting agencies may also find it difficult to quickly determine an arrestee's eligibility for collection in the field, particularly if their state's list of qualifying offenses is extensive and complex.

Linked criminal justice information systems, along with routine training, can help collecting agencies determine when they need to collect a sample and increase the likelihood that laboratories will receive all eligible samples. These systems also can alert laboratory staff responsible

for verifying sample eligibility. Of course, if agencies are to rely on data systems to provide them with information regarding sample eligibility, these systems must be kept up to date.

At what point in criminal case processing can a sample be collected or analyzed?

Nearly two-thirds of states in our review authorize DNA collection immediately after arrest, typically at a local booking or detention facility. Although collection at arrest is the norm, 11 states require an arraignment or judicial determination of probable cause to occur before a sample can be collected or analyzed.[13]

Provisions that require a judicial probable cause determination or arraignment ensure the involvement of a judicial officer before a profile is generated for uploading to CODIS.[14] These added protections are not without costs, such as delays in collection and analysis and more work for state agencies. For example, in states that require a judicial probable cause determination before analysis, collecting agencies must gather the sample but wait to send it to the laboratory, or the laboratory must wait to analyze it. In interviews, laboratory administrators in these states described an ongoing need to verify the status of the associated case through either a case processing database or direct communication with the courts. These added steps can lead to bottlenecks in the system and delay sample processing.

Although linked criminal justice information systems could allow agencies to monitor case status regularly and consistently, not all laboratories and collecting agencies have direct access to case processing information. And for those that do have access, laboratory and court data systems may not be designed to exchange information easily. Regular communication about cases among collecting agencies, courts and laboratories may also be challenging for agencies with already limited time and resources.

Who is responsible for collection?

Responsibility for collection is often set in statute. Of the 17 states that designate a specific type of agency in their arrestee DNA legislation, the vast majority designate the arresting agency, booking agent, detention center, sheriff or jail as the primary collector.

The number and variety of unique collecting agencies — which in some states total into the hundreds — can complicate implementation of arrestee DNA laws.[15] Our interviews with laboratory administrators suggest that the sheer number of agencies collecting and submitting DNA samples can present an administrative challenge for laboratories, which are often primarily responsible for administration and training. The need for training varies depending on several factors, including whether:

■ Agencies are new to DNA collection.

■ Technology or data systems have changed or contain new information.

■ Procedures have changed (such as a switch from blood to buccal swab collection or a change in the scope of collection).

Training is likely to be time-intensive for laboratories when an arrestee law is enacted. Moreover, several state laboratories noted that high turnover in collecting agencies has resulted in an ongoing need to train new staff.

Most state laws do not address responsibility for overseeing collection activities in their DNA laws. As a result, oversight functions like training and coordination often fall to laboratory staff. In addition, laboratories are responsible for compliance tasks such as verifying sample eligibility and ensuring that materials are submitted correctly. This administrative role may pose challenges

> Most states place the responsibility for initiating expungement on the individual from whom a sample was collected.

for state laboratories that are largely staffed by skilled analysts — individuals who may not have experience with oversight, training and interagency coordination.

Our research reveals that the time and staff needed to complete administrative duties depend on a variety of factors associated with collection. One such factor is the completeness of collection kits when they arrive at the laboratory — laboratories may encounter kits that are not completed correctly, not completed in a timely manner or missing information that laboratories need to process the sample. Laboratories also report instances where collecting agencies erroneously collect samples from individuals who have not been arrested for a qualifying offense — and others that do not collect arrestee samples at all. Some state laboratories have attempted to gain compliance by monitoring cases that should have resulted in collection and

notifying collecting agencies if the laboratory did not receive a sample. However, it is important to note that although laboratories almost always assume responsibility for oversight of arrestee DNA policies and the costs associated with devoting staff time to administrative tasks, they rarely have the legal authority to compel an agency to comply with rules.

What policies govern the collection and analysis of duplicate samples?

Not all arrestees are new to the criminal justice system.[16] Arrestees who were previously arrested may already have a DNA profile in CODIS. Despite the likelihood that collecting agencies will arrest repeat offenders, only about half of arrestee DNA laws address whether agencies can or should collect samples from people who have a profile in CODIS. Even when such provisions are present, the laws rarely consider the logistical issues that laboratories and collecting agencies may encounter when checking for duplicates.

The collection of duplicate samples can provide some degree of built-in quality control — such as when a duplicate profile matches to the same forensic profile and confirms the original analysis — but it also means that states are expending limited resources to collect samples and create DNA profiles that do not add power to the database. Our interviews indicate that duplicates can represent a significant cost to states, depending on the number of duplicates received (with rough estimates ranging from 5 to 50 percent of total samples) and the costs associated with collection (estimated at $4 to $6 per kit) and analysis (ranging from $20 to $40 per sample). Some states actively seek to minimize duplicates, others choose to include them and still others are unable to identify duplicates.

Minimizing the number of duplicates can be time- and resource-intensive. State crime laboratory administrators note that the number of duplicates that their laboratories receive is influenced by the availability of automated, linked data systems that can quickly inform collecting agencies when a sample needs to be collected. For example, in some states, the computerized criminal history records include a flag that indicates that DNA has already been collected. If an unnecessary sample is collected and submitted for analysis, laboratory staff with access to linked systems can also check to determine whether the incoming sample already has an associated profile in CODIS. Indeed, many of the laboratories that experience high volumes of duplicates do not have the capacity to check for duplicates and may only identify them when two profiles hit against each other in CODIS. Of course, these data systems must contain up-to-date information if they are to be helpful in the field.

Who is responsible for initiating expungement?

In order for an arrestee profile to be uploaded to NDIS, states must have FBI-approved expungement provisions that describe the process for expunging a profile if a qualifying charge is dismissed or results in acquittal. Most states place the responsibility for initiating expungement on the individual from whom a sample was collected. States that bear the responsibility for initiating expungement include Maryland, Missouri, North Carolina, South Carolina, Tennessee, Vermont and Virginia.[17]

These additional provisions, which are intended to protect the rights of arrestees who are not ultimately convicted, often carry increased collection, analysis and monitoring

activities (and, therefore, increased costs). Interviews with laboratory administrators suggest that these increased activities have deterred many states from compelling government agencies to bear the responsibility for initiating expungement. State-initiated expungement processes require a great deal of coordination between the laboratory

> **The sheer volume of samples received may be difficult for laboratories to manage with existing resources.**

and the agency responsible for initiating the expungement process. In some states, the burden of checking for expungement eligibility falls to the laboratory, which requires staff to regularly check case processing information to determine case disposition and may require them to build infrastructure to track case processing events.

Regardless of which criminal justice agency bears the burden of expungement, automatic expungement provisions ensure that only individuals convicted of the offense for which DNA was collected have profiles retained in CODIS. In fact, our interviews with state crime laboratories suggest that when individuals bear the burden of initiating the expungement process, very few expungements actually occur and profiles are retained of individuals who were never formally charged with a qualifying offense or whose case resulted in acquittal

or dismissal. Some states have been proactive about providing information on expungement policies to arrestees to encourage the initiation of expungement procedures. For example, California's Department of Justice works with county jails to ensure that arrestees are advised of their right to request an expungement. Some states, including Kansas and California, offer expungement request forms on their public websites.

Considerations for Legislators

More than half of the states in this country currently authorize the collection of DNA from individuals following arrest or charging; several other states have recently considered similar legislation.

States may face a number of challenges if they implement arrestee DNA legislation. Verifying that a sample is eligible to be collected and analyzed and determining whether the individual has previously provided a sample can be time-consuming for all involved agencies, especially those that are using older data systems. Laboratories in states that require a judicial determination of probable cause or a state-initiated expungement process may also need to expend significant resources monitoring case processing information to determine if an individual has been charged with or convicted of a qualifying offense. And the sheer volume of samples received may be difficult for laboratories to manage with existing resources.

Our research to date, based on the experiences of states that have already instituted arrestee DNA collection laws, strongly suggests that lawmakers who may be contemplating the expansion of DNA collection in their states should consider the system changes that may be required to implement the new policy. Clearly, collecting and analyzing DNA samples from arrestees requires planning, resources and time to support state crime laboratories and collecting agencies. Existing data systems may require integration and automation, and laboratories will likely need additional resources to hire and train staff, develop collecting agency training materials, and design and distribute new collection kits. This need for training will likely be ongoing, in large part due to turnover in collecting agencies. Our findings indicate that developing new systems and materials, training staff, and preparing for new responsibilities will require a period of time to implement — from a few months to a year — depending on the scope of additional responsibilities.

By considering these resource needs in advance, states have the opportunity to alleviate some of the burdens of new arrestee DNA laws on laboratories and collecting agencies and improve the chances for compliance.

About the authors: Julie Samuels is a senior fellow at the Urban Institute's Justice Policy Center and serves as the principal investigator of a project to examine the policies, practices and implications of arrestee DNA collection. Elizabeth Davies, research associate, and Dwight Pope, research assistant, also work on this project in the Justice Policy Center. Ashleigh Holand was a research associate with the Urban Institute at the time of the article's writing.

NCJ 238484

Learn more about DNA backlogs: https://www.ncjrs.gov/pdffiles1/nij/232197.pdf.

Read about DNA databases: http://www.dna.gov/solving-crimes/cold-cases/howdatabasesaid.

Notes

1. See Page, Doug, "New State Law on DNA Leads to Arrest in 10-Year-Old Rape," *Dayton Daily News Online,* November 14, 2011, www.daytondailynews.com/news/crime/new-state-law-on-dna-leads-to-arrest-in-10-year-old-rape-1284425.html; and Heffner, Jessica, "DNA Samples Lead to Arrest of Criminal Suspects," *Dayton Daily News Online,* February 15, 2012, http://www.daytondailynews.com/news/dayton-news/dna-samples-lead-to-arrest-of-criminal-suspects-1329261.html.

2. We use the word "arrestee" to refer to a person whose DNA is eligible for collection following arrest and prior to conviction. It includes individuals whose DNA is collected following arrest, arraignment, indictment or judicial determination of probable cause.

3. Studies of preventable crimes have been conducted in Chicago, Denver, Washington State and Maryland; see http://www.denverda.org/dna/DNA_Arrestee_Database_Cases.htm for more information.

4. Illinois has not been interviewed because it only recently authorized collection at the time of writing this article. South Carolina could not be reached for an interview.

5. LA Rev Stat § 15:609; Acts 1997, No. 737, §1.

6. Pub.L. 109-162 amended 42 U.S.C. § 14132 and § 14135a, permitting states to upload arrestee profiles to NDIS and authorizing federal agencies to collect DNA from arrestees (2006).

7. The median period of time between arrest and adjudication is 92 days (see Cohen, Thomas H., and Tracey Kyckelhahn, *Felony Defendants in Large Urban Counties, 2006,* Washington, D.C.: Bureau of Justice

Statistics, U.S. Department of Justice, 2010, available at http://bjs.ojp.usdoj.gov/content/pub/pdf/fdluc06.pdf). Some states, such as California, also have the authority to retain DNA profiles for a certain period of time following an acquittal or dismissal.

8. Siegel, Jay, and Susan D. Narveson, *Why Arrestee DNA Legislation Can Save Indiana Taxpayers Over $60 Million Per Year,* dnasaves.org, 2009, available at http://dnasaves.org/files/IN_DNA_Cost_Savings_Study.pdf.

9. The Supreme Court of Virginia upheld the arrestee law (*Anderson v. Commonwealth of Virginia,* 650 S.E. 2d 702 (Va.2007)). The Minnesota Court of Appeals found that the Minnesota DNA arrestee statute violates the Fourth Amendment (*In re Welfare of C.T.L.,* 722 N.W.2d (Minn. Ct. App. 2006)). The California arrestee DNA collection law was found unconstitutional by a state appellate court, and the case will be heard before the state's highest court (*People v. Buza,* 129 Cal.Rptr.3d (Cal. Ct. App. 2011) cert. granted, 262 P.3d 854 (Cal. 2011)). In April 2012, the Maryland Supreme Court found the state's arrestee law unconstitutional in *King v. State* (No. 68, 2012 WL 1392636 (Md. Apr. 24, 2012)). Readers interested in learning more about these issues should consult Sarah B. Berson's article, "Debating DNA Collection," *NIJ Journal* 264 (2009): 9-16, available at http://www.nij.gov/journals/264/debating-DNA.htm.

10. Alabama, Alaska, California, Colorado, Florida (by 2019), Kansas, Louisiana, New Mexico (2011), North Dakota, Ohio, South Carolina, South Dakota and Vermont authorize DNA collection from any individual charged with a felony offense. Arizona, Arkansas, Connecticut, Illinois, Maryland, Michigan, Minnesota, Missouri,

New Jersey, North Carolina, Tennessee, Texas, Utah and Virginia authorize collection for a subset of felonies. According to its statute, Oklahoma authorizes collection at arrest from "any alien unlawfully present under federal immigration law." Connecticut authorizes collection from "any person arrested for the commission of a serious felony and, prior to such arrest, [who] has been convicted of a felony but has not submitted to the taking of a blood or other biological sample for DNA (deoxyribonucleic acid) analysis pursuant to this section." In Utah, "a DNA specimen is not required to be obtained if the court determines that obtaining a DNA specimen would create a substantial and unreasonable risk to the health of the person."

11. Alabama, Arizona, Kansas, Louisiana, Minnesota, South Carolina and South Dakota.

12. Provided that the laboratory does not collect duplicate samples from arrested individuals who have already submitted their DNA under existing convicted offender laws.

13. For example, arraignment or a judicial probable cause determination is needed for *collection* in Florida, Illinois, Minnesota, North Carolina, Tennessee, Vermont and Virginia; Texas requires an indictment or waiver of indictment if the arrestee has not been previously convicted of or placed on deferred adjudication for a qualifying offense. Probable cause is needed for *analysis* in Colorado, Maryland, New Mexico (2011) and Utah.

14. In a 1987 study, 23 percent of felony arrests brought by law enforcement for prosecution were never filed in the courts. See Boland, Barbara, Catherine H. Conly, Paul Mahanna, Lynn Warner, and Ronald Sones, *The Prosecution of Felony Arrests, 1987,* Washington, D.C.: Bureau of Justice Statistics, U.S. Department of Justice, 1990, available at https://www.ncjrs.gov/pdffiles1/Digitization/124140NCJRS.pdf.

15. For example, there are more than 500 collecting agencies in Michigan and Ohio.

16. We did not find any national estimates of the proportion of felony arrestees with prior felony convictions. The Bureau of Justice Statistics has reported that 43 percent of felony defendants (i.e., individuals for whom the court has filed formal charges) had been convicted previously of a felony. See Cohen & Kyckelhahn, 2010.

17. Minnesota was a "split state," such that cases resulting in acquittal would be automatically expunged, while cases resulting in dismissal would require the individual to initiate expungement. Given the volume of cases that resulted in dismissal (compared to acquittals), the individual would be responsible for initiating expungement in the majority of cases.

Preventing Children's Exposure to Violence: The Defending Childhood Initiative

by Sarah B. Berson, Jolene Hernon and Beth Pearsall

An NIJ-funded evaluation takes a close look at communities developing strategies to address childhood exposure to violence.

Sixty percent of American children are exposed to violence, crime or abuse in their homes, schools and communities.[1] Children exposed to violence — whether as victims or as witnesses — are more likely to exhibit aggressive behavior, such as bullying and fighting in school, and they are at higher risk of engaging in criminal behavior later in life by repeating the violence they experienced as children.[2]

Yet there is hope. Research has found that early identification and intervention, along with continued follow-up, can help prevent or reduce the impact of exposure to violence.[3]

To help address the problem of children's exposure to violence, U.S. Attorney General Eric Holder launched the Defending Childhood Initiative in 2010. The Initiative's goals are to:

- Prevent children's exposure to violence.

- Mitigate the negative impact of children's exposure to violence when it does occur.

- Develop knowledge and spread awareness about children's exposure to violence.

To pursue these goals, the Department of Justice awarded $1.25 million to develop and evaluate innovative programs. Eight project demonstration sites were selected to develop, implement and test plans designed to reduce children's exposure to violence in

their communities.[4] NIJ-funded researchers at the Center for Court Innovation are rigorously evaluating the sites' activities to determine which efforts are effective. The evaluations will help researchers and practitioners to better understand what does and does not work in reducing and mitigating children's exposure to violence, so evidence-based policies and programs can be developed and put into place.

The demonstration program, which is managed by the Department of Justice's Office of Juvenile Justice and Delinquency Prevention, is divided into two phases: Phase I — Assessment and Strategic Planning, and Phase II — Implementation and Evaluation.

Phase I: Assessment and Strategic Planning

During Phase I, which ended in April 2011, the demonstration sites conducted assessments to identify community needs. They developed strategic plans and proposed methods for preventing children's exposure to violence, treating the psychological effects of such exposure, and increasing awareness of youth violence and resources. Specific strategies included:

■ Bringing a wide range of stakeholders (politicians, law enforcement agencies, social service organizations, researchers and school representatives) together to address children's exposure to violence. Some sites formed new coalitions, and others folded programs into existing coalitions, such as public safety or early childhood collaboratives.

■ Establishing new or enhancing existing data collection and analysis systems to better track and analyze incidents reported to law

enforcement and child protective services, arrest rates, and related data from schools and other agencies.[5]

■ Implementing evidence-based curricula in schools on dating violence prevention and healthy relationships.

■ Using a trauma-informed practice checklist to monitor agency compliance with evidence-based practices.

■ Educating school, mental health and medical professionals, as well as parents and advocates, on identifying and understanding the impact of children's exposure to violence.

■ Training teachers, school staff and school leaders on evidence-based, trauma-focused mental health interventions.

> ## Findings from the Comprehensive National Survey on Children's Exposure to Violence
>
> ■ Sixty percent of American children were exposed to violence, crime or abuse in their homes, schools and communities.
>
> ■ Almost 40 percent of American children were direct victims of two or more violent acts, and 1 in 10 were victims of violence five or more times.
>
> ■ Children were more likely to be exposed to violence and crime than adults.
>
> ■ Almost 1 in 10 American children saw one family member assault another family member, and more than 25 percent had been exposed to family violence during their lifetime.
>
> ■ Exposure to one type of violence increased the likelihood that a child would be exposed to other types of violence and exposed multiple times.
>
> ---
>
> **Note:** Finkelhor, David, Heather Turner, Richard Ormrod, Sherry Hamby, and Kristen Kracke, "Children's Exposure to Violence: A Comprehensive National Survey," *Juvenile Justice Bulletin* (October 2009), Washington, D.C.: U.S. Department of Justice, Office of Justice Programs, Office of Juvenile Justice and Delinquency Prevention, available at http://www.ncjrs.gov/pdffiles1/ojjdp/227744.pdf.

■ Training tribe elders/Peacemakers to work directly with youth to address violence and proper behavior within the tribal region.

Formative Evaluation of Phase I

The Center for Court Innovation conducted a formative evaluation of Phase I activities.[6] Formative evaluations are conducted while programs or initiatives are still in development. Unlike evaluations of programs after they are implemented, which assess programs in terms of their processes, impacts, and costs and benefits, formative evaluations describe the planning process; assess goals and objectives met during development; and identify potential strengths, weaknesses and opportunities, as well as barriers to implementation and adaptation. They also document lessons learned and strategies used over the course of the development process. Collecting and disseminating this kind of information can help jurisdictions interested in replicating the programs in the future.

The Center for Court Innovation's goals for the formative evaluation of Phase I were to:

- Implement a participatory research process with all sites.

- Describe key strategies, outcomes and available data.

- Produce evaluability assessments for each site and an evaluation design for Phase II (implementation).

All of the sites proposed some mix of prevention, intervention and public awareness strategies. Sites varied, however, in a number of ways — including geography, demography, level of violence, research expertise, existing infrastructure and history of collaborating with key stakeholders from other sectors. In their strategic proposals, the sites developed approaches that fit the particular needs and resources of their communities. For example, two sites that identified domestic violence as the most common form of violence to which children were exposed in their communities created a proposal to implement evidence-based curricula on dating violence prevention and forming healthy relationships. One of these sites is including this dating violence curriculum as part of a universal prevention strategy. After forging relationships with local school districts, the site proposed using schools, daycare and other existing programs to reach children 17 and younger with a wide variety of primary prevention programming. Examples of other strategies developed by the sites are listed above and in the Phase I Evaluation report.

The evaluators also identified some common themes among the proposed strategies. For example, most sites included intensive direct training of service providers and plans for better data systems to improve data collection and more efficiently and systematically track services. Collecting, accessing and sharing data was a challenge for most of the sites.

Phase II: Implementation and Evaluation

Phase II began in October 2011, when the sites started to put their proposed plans into action. It will run until September 2013.

The Center for Court Innovation, with funds from NIJ, will evaluate implementation at the demonstration sites. Evaluating implementation at the demonstration sites will allow future sites to learn from their broad range of techniques and approaches for reducing the number of children exposed to violence and mitigating the impact on those already exposed. Researchers will conduct a process evaluation and an impact evaluation.

Process evaluation: The process evaluation will provide a rich account of strategies undertaken at six sites.[7] The evaluation will clarify:

- Why the strategies were chosen

- The scope of each strategy in terms of target population (e.g., geographic, demographic)

- Which agencies were involved

- How implementation unfolded over time

- What barriers to implementation arose and how they were overcome

- The successes, challenges and lessons learned

- How other jurisdictions could replicate the strategy

Impact evaluation: The impact evaluation will show change over time in a number of indicators related to children's exposure to violence. Using a large pre-post community survey (that is, a survey conducted before implementation and again after implementation) at each site, researchers will be able to track changes in adults' attitudes toward violence, perceptions of violence as a community problem, awareness of local resources and knowledge about the effects exposure to violence has on children.[8] Additionally, the researchers will work with sites to access local law enforcement, child welfare services and school incident data, as well as service utilization data, both historically and over the course of the initiative. They will use these data to investigate the associations between the implementation schedule, strategy scope and changes over time. In addition, the researchers will conduct a pre-post survey of professionals participating in training events for each site to assess changes in knowledge, awareness and practices related to children exposed to violence.

Table 1 depicts the desired outcomes and indicators the demonstration sites and evaluators are likely to use to assess the strategies' effectiveness in their communities.

The Defending Childhood Initiative is designed to help communities develop, test and evaluate strategies in the field to determine what works for reducing the number of children exposed to violence. A final report from the research team is expected in 2014.

About the authors: Sarah B. Berson is the managing editor of the *NIJ Journal*. Jolene Hernon is Director of NIJ's Office of Communications. Beth Pearsall is a freelance writer and frequent contributor to the *NIJ Journal*.

NCJ 238485

Table 1. Desired Impacts/Outcomes and Indicators of Success

	Impacts/Outcomes	Indicators
Prevention	Reduced exposure to school violence	• Incidence of bullying • Incidence of physical fights/threats at school • Incidence of disciplinary suspensions
	Reduced exposure to violence at home	• Incidence of child abuse, neglect, etc. • Incidence of domestic violence (with child present) • Incidence of relative/sibling violence
	Reduced exposure to community violence	• Incidence of violent crime (adult/juvenile) • Child/juvenile victims of violence
	Increased healthy relationship knowledge, attitudes, behavior and resilience factors	• Increased knowledge of healthy relationships • Improved healthy relationship attitudes • Improved healthy relationship behaviors
Intervention	Increased/improved screening for children exposed to violence	• Incidence of screening for children exposed to violence • Use of standardized screening tools
	Improved systems responses for children exposed to violence	• Changes in systems, policies and procedures • Increased collaboration among agencies • Increased information/data sharing
	Improved treatment outcomes and resilience factors for children exposed to violence	• Reduced negative symptoms • Increased resilience factors
Awareness	Increased awareness of effects of children's exposure to violence	• Increased knowledge of effects of children's exposure to violence • Increased negative attitudes toward children's exposure to violence
	Increased awareness of community resources/services available for children exposed to violence	• Increased knowledge of resources • Increased likelihood to use/recommend resources
	Increased awareness of what constitutes violence	• Increased knowledge of what constitutes violence • Increased negative attitudes toward all types of violence/ acceptance of violence

For more information:

■ Read the Formative Evaluation of the Phase I Demonstration Program at http://www.courtinnovation. org/sites/default/files/documents/ Defending_Childhood_Initiative.pdf.

■ Visit the Defending Childhood Initiative's website, http://www. justice.gov/defendingchildhood.

Notes

1. Finkelhor, David, Heather Turner, Richard Ormrod, Sherry Hamby, and Kristen Kracke, "Children's Exposure to Violence: A Comprehensive National Survey," *Juvenile Justice Bulletin* (October 2009), Washington, D.C.: U.S. Department of Justice, Office of Justice Programs, Office of Juvenile Justice and Delinquency Prevention, available at http://www.ncjrs.gov/ pdffiles1/ojjdp/227744.pdf. Additional information on the survey and related publications are available at http://www. unh.edu/ccrc/projects/natscev.html.

2. Ibid.

3. Ibid.

4. The Phase I demonstration sites were: Boston, Mass.; Cuyahoga County Board of Commissioners, Ohio; Grand Forks, N.D.; Multnomah County Department of Human Services, Ore.; Portland, Maine; Shelby County, Tenn.; the Chippewa Cree Tribe (Mont.); and the Rosebud Sioux Tribe (S.D.).

5. The comprehensiveness of existing data varies greatly by type of violence, which makes it difficult to accurately and effectively address violence issues. Filling the gaps in existing data would improve accuracy and effectiveness. Moreover, interagency agreements and mechanisms to build data capacity can improve collection of existing data.

6. Swaner, Rachel, and Julia Kohn, "The U.S. Attorney General's Defending Childhood Initiative: Formative Evaluation of the Phase 1 Demonstration Program," Final report to the National Institute of Justice, grant number 2010-IJ-CX-0015, November 2011, NCJ 236563, available at https://www.ncjrs.gov/pdffiles1/nij/ grants/236563.pdf.

7. Multnomah County Department of Human Services (Ore.) and Portland, Maine, were not selected to receive full implementation funding and will not undergo Phase II evaluation.

8. Because of the Shelby County, Tenn., site's unique methodology (a place-based approach focused on several apartment complexes), researchers will not implement a community survey at this site. Instead, they will develop an alternative strategy to assess similar variables at this site.

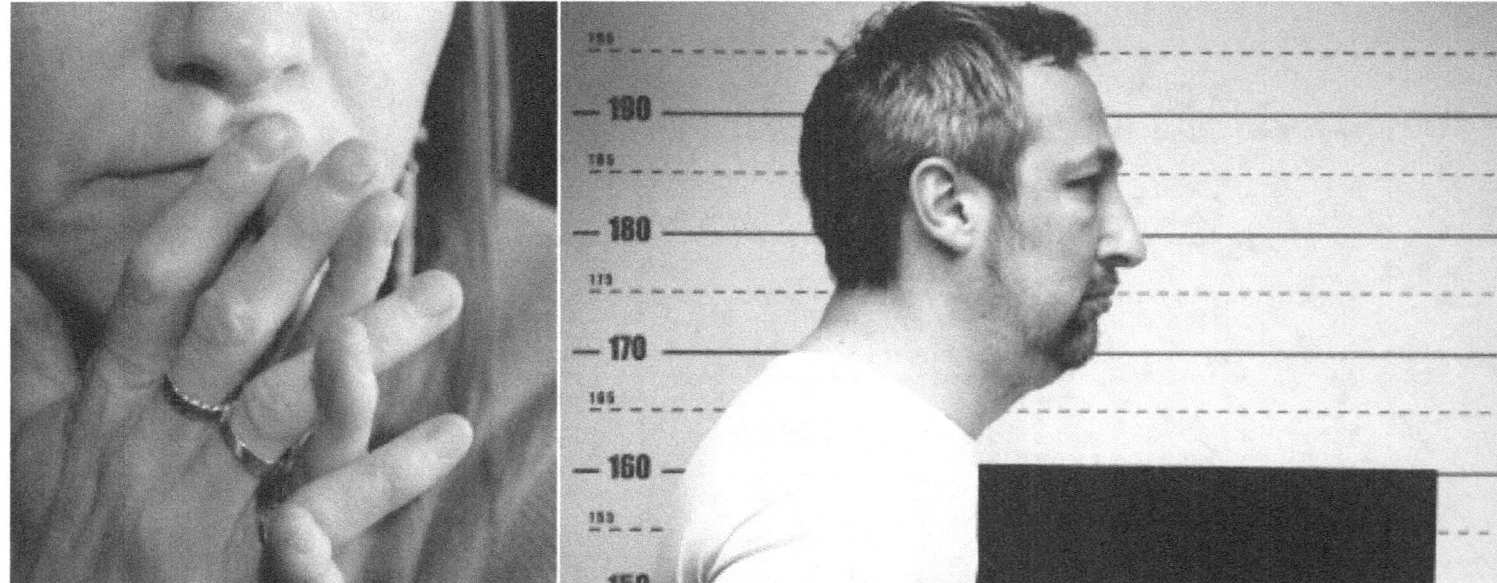

To Err Is Human: Using Science to Reduce Mistaken Eyewitness Identifications in Police Lineups

by Maureen McGough

Researchers take police lineup studies from the laboratory to the field.

In 1984, *a Cook County, Ill., jury found 27-year-old Ronnie Bullock guilty of raping a 9-year-old girl in Chicago's south side. He was sentenced to 60 years in prison. Crucial to the prosecution's case was the victim's identification of Bullock in a police lineup. A second rape victim — a 12-year-old girl — also viewed a police lineup and identified Bullock as her attacker.[1]*

Maintaining his innocence, Bullock sought relief from the courts. His conviction was upheld on appeal in 1987, and two state postconviction petitions were unsuccessful. Bullock's federal habeas petition was denied in 1991.[2]

In June of 1993, he was granted a motion to have impounded evidence released for DNA testing. Tests revealed that Bullock was not the source of the semen found on the victim's clothing, and a judge dismissed the charges against him in 1994.[3]

Bullock spent 10 and a half years in prison for a crime he did not commit.[4]

Nationwide, mistaken eyewitness identifications have played a role in 75 percent of convictions later overturned because of DNA evidence,[5] and criminal justice practitioners and researchers have a pervasive interest in finding ways to improve the methods used for eyewitness identifications. A good deal of research has focused on the police lineup, in which victims and witnesses attempt to distinguish a suspect from other individuals presented (known as "fillers").

A recent study from the American Judicature Society (AJS) is adding to the body of research by investigating which lineup method results in fewer mistaken identifications:[6]

■ Sequential, in which the witness views lineup members one at a time and makes a decision on each individual member, or

■ Simultaneous, in which the witness views the entire lineup at once

Past research using controlled laboratory experiments consistently showed that sequential methods yielded fewer mistaken identifications. But in 2006, a field study in Illinois called into question the superiority of the sequential method (and with it, the use of controlled laboratory experiments as approximations for actual eyewitnesses to crimes).

Scientists, however, identified flaws in the Illinois study's design and implementation. As a result, some experts have deemed the results "difficult or impossible to interpret."[7]

To produce more rigorous data using field techniques rather than laboratory techniques, the AJS research team developed an improved research design for its study.

> The "Greensboro Protocols" emphasized the importance of true random assignment and the consistent use of double-blind lineups for conducting a scientifically sound field experiment.

The initial report on the AJS study indicates that sequential lineups significantly reduce the number of filler identifications without significantly reducing the number of accurate positive identifications. Thus, the AJS findings support results from past laboratory experiments.

Research From Laboratories to the Field

Given the vital role of eyewitness testimony in the administration of justice and the inherent risks therein, extensive research has been dedicated to developing lineups that minimize identification of fillers without significantly reducing accurate, positive identifications.

However, many of the variables that may affect the accuracy of eyewitness identification are out of the control of the criminal justice system.[8] These include lighting of the crime scene; length of time a witness was exposed to the perpetrator; severity of the crime; and characteristics of the witness and perpetrator, such as race, age and sex. These variables are helpful in estimating the likely accuracy of eyewitness

identification, but they cannot be controlled in actual criminal cases.[9]

Several renowned eyewitness researchers have focused studies on variables that the criminal justice system could control, such as who administers the lineup, how the lineup is administered, lineup compositions and instructions given to witnesses.[10]

By focusing on these controllable variables, researchers have produced findings from laboratory experiments that shape investigative practices and procedures.[11] These science-based practices include:

■ Using fillers in lineups that match the verbal description of the perpetrator

■ Informing the witness that the perpetrator may or may not be present in the lineup

■ Using a double-blind administration in which the lineup administrator does not know who the suspect is and therefore is unable to transmit inadvertent cues or feedback to the identifying witness[12]

Laboratory tests also show that sequential lineups offer a better ratio of accurate to mistaken identifications than simultaneous lineups. Sequential lineups require witnesses to compare each individual they see to their recollection of the suspect.[13] This increases accuracy and reduces the risk that witnesses will make a judgment based on a relative comparison of who among the group looks most like the perpetrator relative to the other lineup members. In fact, when a double-blind lineup was administered using the sequential technique in laboratory testing, identifications were twice as reliable as those from traditional lineups.[14]

The Supreme Court and Eyewitness Testimony — Perry v. New Hampshire

Eyewitness testimony plays a crucial role in the American criminal justice system. However, like any process relying on the integrity of human memory, eyewitness testimony is imperfect. The American Judicature Society study found that even when lineups were conducted using procedures shown to lead to fewer mistaken identifications, witnesses identified a "filler" 12.2 percent of the time. The courts must therefore strike a balance between allowing the introduction of eyewitness testimony that can be crucial to the prosecution's case and protecting defendants from unreasonably unreliable evidence.

The Supreme Court has long held that it is up to jurors to evaluate eyewitness testimony and make their own judgments as to its credibility. However, the Court has also held that the Constitution's Due Process Clause requires preliminary judicial inquiry into the reliability of eyewitness identification if law enforcement created unnecessarily suggestive circumstances during the identification. In Perry v. New Hampshire, the petitioner asked the Court to apply the same principle — that

identifications made under suggestive conditions require preliminary judicial inquiry — when happenstance renders the identification setting suggestive.

In Perry, a New Hampshire police officer responded to a call that an African American man was attempting to break into cars in a nearby lot. When the officer asked an eyewitness to describe the man, she pointed to Perry — the only African American man standing in the lot next to a police officer — and identified him as the man in question. Perry's arrest followed. The out-of-court identification was introduced at trial and Perry was found guilty of theft.

In its October 2011 opinion, the Court held that the introduction of this out-of-court identification did not violate the Due Process Clause. The Court said that the determination of the credibility of the testimony in question should be left to the jurors and declined to put what it deemed new legal limits on the use of questionable eyewitness testimony at trial. The Court also opined that Perry's

argument would open the door to judicial preview of most — if not all — eyewitness identifications.

Justice Sonia Sotomayor was the lone dissenter. Although the majority held that the crucial, common factor in relevant Court precedent was that police arranged a suggestive interview, Justice Sotomayor countered that the suggestive nature of the interview itself — not the circumstances that led the suggestive nature — was the key. She believed that the majority opinion did not adequately consider empirical evidence showing mistaken identifications as the single greatest cause of wrongful convictions in this country. She also highlighted studies showing that eyewitness recollections are highly susceptible to distortion and that jurors overestimate the accuracy of eyewitness identifications.

The 2006 Illinois Report

Although laboratory results were promising, proposed changes in investigative practices needed to be field tested before they could be used to support widespread procedural overhauls. In 2003, the Illinois state legislature charged the Illinois State Police with conducting a yearlong field test of the effectiveness of the sequential,

double-blind lineup compared with the traditional (non-blind, simultaneous) lineup.[15]

The results were surprising. In 2006, the Illinois State Police released a report (often referred to as The Mecklenberg Report after its author, Sheri Mecklenberg) showing that, in two of the three jurisdictions participating in the study,

double-blind, sequential lineups produced a higher rate of identification of innocent fillers and a lower rate of identification of suspects.[16] In other words, this report contradicted what laboratory experiments had shown for years, and it recommended against instituting changes based solely on laboratory science.[17] The report, which was widely publicized, drew resolute support and severe criticism, particularly regarding the design and implementation of the study.[18]

First and foremost, critics stressed that the study confounded the simultaneous/sequential and non-blind/double-blind variables, rendering results largely uninterpretable. It was impossible to determine whether the better outcome using the simultaneous lineups was partly or entirely attributable to the influence of the non-blind administrator.[19] Notably, some proponents of the study felt that confounding these variables did not color the results, citing research that compared double-blind conditions to non-blind conditions and finding no effects.[20]

Additionally, critics cited the fact that cases were not randomly assigned to either group, and cases thought to be "tougher," such as cross-race identifications or those in which the lineup took place after a delay, were more likely to be assigned to the sequential group, thus negatively skewing the sequential results.[21] Critics also noted that some filler identifications were not recorded in simultaneous lineups, thus positively skewing the simultaneous results.[22]

The Greensboro Protocols

To address critiques of The Mecklenberg Report, the AJS convened scientists, lawyers, prosecutors and police in Greensboro, N.C., to develop a set of guidelines for conducting field experiments testing the simultaneous/sequential variable. The group was committed to conducting field research that would gather reliable data on the administration of the lineup and witness and event variables. Data determined to be essential for a scientifically sound field experiment included time between crime and lineup, type of crime, whether

a weapon was present, viewing conditions, sobriety of the witness, certainty of the witness, and whether it was a cross-race identification.[23]

The "Greensboro Protocols" emphasized the importance of true random assignment of lineups into the sequential or simultaneous groups, and the consistent use of double-blind lineups in both groups was also deemed essential for conducting a scientifically sound field experiment.

The protocols also highlighted the importance of using computers — both for administering the lineups and for recording witness responses — to ensure that procedures were fairly conducted in accordance with best practices. Computers were deemed especially important because they could ensure uniform administration of lineups according to protocol, randomly assign lineups as either sequential or simultaneous, and randomly order the photos within a lineup. Computers would also allow for uniform, reliable and complete recordings of witness responses, including the time it took for witnesses to make a determination.

The AJS Field Study

Relying on the Greensboro Protocols, the AJS developed a field experiment that compensated for the deficiencies of the 2006 Illinois study. The field experiment was conducted at four sites: the Austin Police Department (Texas), the Charlotte-Mecklenburg Police Department (N.C.), the San Diego Police Department (Calif.) and the Tucson Police Department (Ariz.).

The AJS research team excluded lineups that were not conducted using a double-blind procedure, as

well as lineups in which the eyewitness had prior knowledge of the suspect through a previous acquaintance. This left researchers with 497 protocol-consistent lineups for crimes, ranging from simple assault to murder.

Results

There were no significant differences in a witness's ability to identify the suspect between the simultaneous and sequential techniques. Witnesses identified the suspect 25.5 percent of the time in simultaneous lineups and 27.3 percent of the time in sequential lineups. This small difference in identification rates falls within the margin of error and should not be considered a meaningful difference.

However, simultaneous lineups resulted in 18.1 percent identification of fillers, whereas sequential lineups resulted in 12.2 percent identification of fillers. This 5.9 percent difference in filler identifications was found to be statistically significant.

The AJS study results are consistent with the results of decades of laboratory tests showing that sequential lineups reduce mistaken identifications without significantly reducing accurate identifications.

Next Steps

Researchers plan to conduct additional analyses of the data to determine:

■ Whether witnesses are more certain about their mistaken identifications in sequential or simultaneous lineups

■ Whether accuracy changes with the witness's status as a victim or bystander

■ Whether the identifications were same-race or cross-race

Additionally, although identifications of fillers are clearly erroneous, identifications of the suspect are not necessarily accurate because the suspect is not always the perpetrator. The Police Foundation is leading a second phase of research to follow up on this area.

The police lineup is an inherently human process, and therefore inherently flawed. Although no single study can lead to the development of a procedure guaranteeing consistently accurate identifications, a well-designed field study can be an important step in developing best practices for lineups and other identification practices.

About the author: Maureen McGough is an attorney and NIJ's outreach coordinator.

NCJ 238486

For more information:

- Mecklenberg, Sheri H., *Report to the Legislature of the State of Illinois: The Illinois Pilot Program on Sequential Double-Blind Identification Procedures,* Springfield, IL: Illinois State Police, 2006, http://www.chicagopolice.org/IL%20Pilot%20on%20Eyewitness%20ID.pdf

- Wells, Gary L., Nancy K. Steblay, and Jennifer E. Dysart, *A Test of the Simultaneous vs. Sequential Lineup Methods: An Initial Report of the AJS National Eyewitness Identification Field Studies,* Des Moines, IA: American Judicature Society, 2011, http://www.ajs.org/wc/pdfs/EWID_PrintFriendly.pdf

Notes

1. Conners, Edward, Thomas Lundregan, Neal Miller, and Tom McEwen, "Convicted by Juries, Exonerated by Science: Case Studies in the Use of DNA Evidence to Establish Innocence After Trial," Final report to the National Institute of Justice, grant number OJP-95-215, June 1996, NCJ 161258, available at https://www.ncjrs.gov/pdffiles/dnaevid.pdf.

2. Garrett, Brandon L., "Judging Innocence," *Columbia Law Review* 108 (2008): 65, http://www.columbialawreview.org/assets/pdfs/108/1/Garrett.pdf.

3. Conners, "Convicted by Juries, Exonerated by Science," 40.

4. Ibid.

5. The Innocence Project, "Eyewitness Misidentification," http://www.innocenceproject.org/understand/Eyewitness-Misidentification.php.

6. One of the four study sites, Tucson, Ariz., was initially funded as a standalone field study by NIJ. The results of that site analysis were included in the AJS Field Study after the NIJ study received funding to use laptop computers.

7. Schacter, Daniel L., Robin Dawes, Larry L. Jacoby, Daniel Kahneman, Richard Lempert, Henry L. Roediger, and Robert Rosenthal, "Policy Forum: Studying Eyewitness Investigations in the Field," *Law and Human Behavior* 32 (2008): 3-5, http://www.jjay.cuny.edu/extra/policyforum.pdf; see generally Conners, "Convicted by Juries, Exonerated by Science."

8. Wells, Gary L., "Applied Eyewitness-Testimony Research: System Variables and Estimator Variables," *Journal of Personality and Social Psychology* 36 (1978): 1546-1557, http://www.psychology.iastate.edu/~glwells/Wells_articles_pdf/Applied_Eyewitness-Testimony_Research.pdf.

9. Ibid., 1548.

10. See, for example, Doyle, James M., "Learning From Error in American Criminal Justice," *The Journal of Criminal Law & Criminology* 100 (2010): 109-148, http://www.law.northwestern.edu/jclc/backissues/v100/n1/1001_109.Doyle.pdf.

11. Ibid., 116.

12. Ibid., 17.

13. Schacter, "Policy Forum."

14. Steblay, Nancy, Jennifer Dysart, Solomon Fulero, and R.C.L. Lindsay, "Eyewitness Accuracy Rates in Sequential and Simultaneous Lineup Presentations: A Meta-Analytic Comparison," *Law and Human Behavior* 25 (2001): 459-473, http://citeseerx.ist.psu.edu/viewdoc/summary?doi=10.1.1.110.8546.

15. Mecklenberg, Sheri H., *Report to the Legislature of the State of Illinois: The Illinois Pilot Program on Sequential Double-Blind Identification Procedures,* Springfield, IL: Illinois State Police, 2006, http://www.chicagopolice.org/IL%20Pilot%20on%20Eyewitness%20ID.pdf.

16. Ibid.

17. Schacter, "Policy Forum."

18. Ibid., 2.

19. Ibid.

20. Malpass, Roy S., "Notes on the Illinois Pilot Program on Sequential Double-Blind Lineup Procedures," *Public Interest Law Reporter* 2006: 5-8, 39-47; See also Ebbesen, Ebbe B., "Comments on IL Simultaneous v. Sequential Lineup Field Test," 2006.

21. Wells, Gary L., Nancy K. Steblay, and Jennifer E. Dysart, *A Test of the Simultaneous vs. Sequential Lineup Methods: An Initial Report of the AJS National Eyewitness Identification Field Studies,* Des Moines, IA: American Judicature Society, 2011, http://www.ajs.org/wc/pdfs/EWID_PrintFriendly.pdf.

22. Ibid.

23. Ibid., ix.

 **www.** *Learn more about the science behind police lineups: http://www.nij.gov/journals/258/police-lineups.html.*

Geography, Spatial Analytics and Technology:

NIJ's Mapping and Analysis for Public Safety Program

Crime mapping sits at the nexus of geography, social science and a variety of other disciplines. Analysts map crime using geographic data, conduct analysis and report the results using cartographic products. By combining an array of data with cartographic techniques and statistical methods, analysts can find solutions to complex social issues. Crime mapping can suggest ways to better deploy law enforcement officers, use public safety resources more efficiently, devise stronger crime-prevention techniques and obtain greater insight into crime.

The Evolution of Crime Mapping at NIJ

NIJ's initial crime mapping endeavors resulted in the creation of the Crime Mapping Research Center, which focused on spreading the use of computerized mapping and surveyed police departments to learn how they were using analytic mapping techniques. NIJ found that law enforcement officers had a significant interest in understanding how geospatial tools and geography could help reduce and prevent crime. NIJ also determined that training would help law enforcement make better use of tools that collect and use geographic information. This led to NIJ's supporting geographic information system

(GIS) training programs to teach law enforcement officers how to capture, analyze, store and present spatial data. GIS allows users to examine how geography affects crime, as well as other topics, including urban planning, emergency services and home foreclosures.

In 2002, the Crime Mapping Research Center evolved into the Mapping and Analysis for Public Safety (MAPS) program, which focused on mapping tools and the use of spatial analysis techniques. Four years later, MAPS shifted its focus to emphasize place-based theories while still helping agencies use GIS to enhance public safety.

MAPS Research

NIJ's MAPS program funds research that uses GIS technologies to statistically analyze spatial data, which leads to a better understanding of crime, more effective deployment of police and use of public safety resources, and stronger crime policies.

The fiscal year 2012 MAPS solicitation contained both theoretical and applied research approaches. Specifically, the solicitation sought proposals for research on how microplace and micro-time strategies (e.g., risk-terrain modeling, CompStat programs and hot spot tactical deployment) are informed, supported or enhanced by criminological theory.

Past NIJ research has produced:

- CrimeStat, a spatial statistical program used to analyze crime locations and hot spots

- An iOS and Droid technology-based crime mapping application developed to help law enforcement officers understand spatial and temporal crime patterns

- A mobile application that uses semiautomated 3D geocoding of Large Urban Structures (e.g., buildings, hallways, elevators and stairways) to deploy effective emergency response and communication

NIJ's MAPS program is currently conducting intramural research on grid cell sizes and a multimethod exploration of hot spot techniques.

▶ Visit NIJ's crime mapping topic pages: http://www.nij.gov/nij/maps/welcome.htm.

▶ Read *Geography and Public Safety:* http://www.nij.gov/nij/maps/bulletin.htm.

▶ The Eleventh Crime Mapping Research Conference (CMRC), held in October 2011, focused on "Crime, Social Ills and Place-Based Solutions" and promoted discussions on neighborhoods and crime, foreclosures, mortgage fraud, and other social ills. See examples of winning posters from the 2011 CMRC poster contest: http://nij.gov/journals/270/maps.htm.

Sleep Disorders, Work Shifts and Officer Wellness

by Beth Pearsall

Two recent studies examined the impact of sleep and work schedules on the health and safety of law enforcement officers.

Police work is inherently risky. Law enforcement officers face the constant threat of being attacked, wounded or even killed when confronting suspects or handling other dangerous situations in the line of duty. And the risk of being injured during routine traffic stops or roadside emergencies is all too real.[1] In fact, law enforcement officers have one of the highest rates of on-the-job injury and illness.[2]

But one of the greatest dangers to officers and their overall performance on the job is often overlooked — fatigue.

Law enforcement officers work demanding schedules characterized by long hours, frequent night shifts and substantial overtime. Insufficient rest or irregular sleep patterns — coupled with the stress of the job — can lead to sleep deprivation and possibly sleep disorders. The result can be severe fatigue that degrades officers' cognition, reaction time and alertness and impairs their ability to protect themselves and the communities they serve.

So how common are sleep deprivation and sleep disorders among law enforcement? And what role do demanding work schedules play?

There is a small but growing body of research examining the effects of sleep disorders and shift schedules on police officer health, safety and performance.[3] Two recently

released studies funded by NIJ make important additions to this research effort. The first study examines sleep disorders among law enforcement officers, and the second explores the impact of shift length on officer wellness. The findings from both have critical implications for law enforcement officers and agencies across the nation.

Sleep Disorders Common Among Officers

Sleep disorders, which are typically associated with poor health, performance and safety outcomes, are twice as prevalent among law enforcement officers compared to the general public — and a new study suggests that they remain largely undiagnosed and untreated.[4]

Researchers at Brigham and Women's Hospital examined sleep disorders and how they affected the health and safety of 4,957 state and local law enforcement officers in the United States and Canada. Using online and onsite screenings and monthly follow-up surveys, the researchers found that just over 40 percent of participating officers had at least one sleep disorder, most of which had not been previously diagnosed.

The most common sleep disorder was obstructive sleep apnea, affecting more than one-third of the officers (33.6 percent or 1,666 of 4,597 respondents). Moderate to severe insomnia came in second (6.5 percent or 281 of 4,298 respondents), followed by shift work disorder (defined as "excessive wake time sleepiness and insomnia associated with night work," affecting 5.4 percent or 269 of 4,597 respondents).

"These findings illustrate the necessity of having proper screening instruments available to detect sleep-related problems among police officers," said Brett Chapman, a social science analyst in NIJ's Office of Research and Evaluation. "Not only is this a health and wellness issue, it is also an issue that can lead to performance problems over the course of their careers."

Having any type of sleep disorder was linked to an increased risk of physical and mental health conditions, including diabetes, depression and cardiovascular disease. The

> ### Sleep disorders are twice as prevalent among police officers compared to the general public.

researchers also found that officers with sleep disorders were more likely than their peers to make serious administrative errors or safety violations, fall asleep while driving, and experience "uncontrolled anger" toward suspects.

But the potential risks to officers — and the general public — due to fatigue are even more common than these findings suggest. According to the researchers, excessive sleepiness is common among police officers, whether they have sleep disorders or not. In fact, almost half of all participants (45.9 percent) reported having fallen asleep while driving. Approximately one-quarter

(26.1 percent) reported that this occurs one to two times per month.

"This [finding] is despite police officers apparently recognizing the dangers associated with drowsy driving," the researchers wrote. "In a survey of North American police officers, almost 90 percent regarded drowsy driving to be as dangerous as drunk driving."

What Role Does Shift Length Play?

Long hours and demanding work schedules have often been cited as major contributors to officer fatigue and health problems. Traditionally, most police departments placed officers on a 40-hour workweek; officers worked 8-hour shifts for five consecutive days, followed by two days off. In recent years, however, an increasing number of agencies have moved to a compressed work schedule in which officers work, for example, four 10-hour shifts or three 12-hour shifts.

But despite the popularity of this trend, few — if any — rigorous scientific studies have examined the advantages and disadvantages of compressed work schedules for officers and agencies.

"It's clear that agencies of all sizes are increasingly departing from the traditional 40-hour workweek and implementing some type of compressed work schedule," said Karen Amendola, Chief Operating Officer at the Police Foundation. "But what's not clear is the scientific basis for these changes."

"Most of the evidence concerning the benefits — and drawbacks — of a compressed work schedule has been anecdotal up to this point," Amendola added. "The few studies that have been conducted either have methodological flaws or were designed in a way that precludes conclusions about cause and effect. Consequently, agencies are scrambling for information."

To help bring some scientific evidence into the scheduling discussion, Amendola and her colleagues at the Police Foundation conducted a randomized controlled experiment that examined how shift work affects officer performance, safety, health, quality of life, fatigue and extra-duty employment.[5] The researchers randomly assigned 275 officers in Detroit, Mich., and Arlington, Texas, to work three types of shifts for six months: five consecutive 8-hour days, four consecutive 10-hour days and three consecutive 12-hour days. The work included day, evening and midnight shifts.

The researchers found that 10-hour shifts offered numerous benefits over the traditionally used 8-hour shifts: Officers get more sleep, report a significantly higher quality of work life and work less overtime.

Sleep and Fatigue. Officers working 10-hour shifts got significantly more sleep per night (more than a half hour) than those working 8-hour shifts, according to the researchers.

"This unique advantage to the 10-hour shift was surprising," admitted Amendola. "Getting a half hour more of sleep a night translates into gaining over 150 hours of sleep a year. This has tremendous implications for police officers' health and on-the-job safety."

Officers working the 12-hour shifts reported greater levels of sleepiness and lower levels of alertness at work than those assigned to 8-hour shifts. The researchers noted that because people often underestimate their level of fatigue and because previous research has shown that risk for accidents increases with number of hours worked, caution should be used when considering adopting 12-hour shifts.

"Not only is this a health and wellness issue, it is also an issue that can lead to performance problems over the course of their careers."

Although there were significant differences in the amount of sleep officers got across the three shifts, the researchers found no significant differences in the quality of sleep or in reported sleep disorders.

Quality of Work Life. The data revealed no significant differences in the quality of officers' personal lives among the three shifts. However, officers working 10-hour shifts reported significantly higher quality of work life than those on 8-hour shifts. No quality of work life benefits resulted from the 12-hour shifts.

Overtime. According to the researchers, officers on 8-hour shifts worked more than five times as much overtime as those on

10-hour shifts, and more than three times as much as those on 12-hour shifts. Reduced levels of overtime for officers working compressed schedules could lead to possible cost savings for agencies.

Additional Outcomes. The results revealed no significant differences among the three shift lengths on work performance, health or work-family conflict.

More Research Needed

Law enforcement officers will continue to face dangerous and stressful situations in the line of duty. Many risks are obvious — for example, gun violence and vehicle accidents. But other dangers — like fatigue — remain hidden. These all-too-common dangers can greatly hinder performance and threaten the safety of both officers and the public.

"We are all trying to keep officers and our communities safe," said Amendola. "These studies mark a good step in that direction. The findings have broad implications for law enforcement officers and agencies across the country."

"But at the same time, a lot more research is needed," she continued. "There are still questions concerning schedules and officer safety that need to be examined."

The researchers at Brigham and Women's Hospital agree. In their sleep disorder study, they call for additional research "to determine whether sleep disorder prevention, screening and treatment programs in occupational settings will reduce these risks."

"Both studies represent NIJ's continued commitment to officer safety, performance and wellness," said Chapman. "It is our hope that the findings from this research will provide practitioners with information that will allow them to make informed decisions that are beneficial to the health and well-being of their officers."

About the author: Beth Pearsall is a freelance writer and frequent contributor to the *NIJ Journal*.

NCJ 238487

 *To learn more about police shift work, visit NIJ's topic page at http://www.nij.gov/nij/topics/ law-enforcement/officer-safety/ stress-fatigue/shift-work.htm.*

Notes

1. For more information, see Pearsall, Beth, "Keeping Officers Safe on the Road," *NIJ Journal* 265 (2010): 10-15, available at http://www.nij.gov/nij/ journals/265/officers.htm.

2. Bureau of Labor Statistics, *Occupational Outlook Handbook, 2010–11 Edition,* Washington, D.C.: U.S. Department of Labor, Bureau of Labor Statistics, available at http:// www.bls.gov/oco/ocos160.htm.

3. See, for example, Vila, Bryan, "Tired Cops: Probable Connections Between Fatigue and the Performance, Health and Safety of Patrol Officers," *American Journal of Police* 15 (1996): 51-92; Vila, Bryan, Gregory B. Morrison, and Dennis J. Kenney, "Improving Shift Schedule and Work-Hour Policies and Practices to Increase Police Officer Performance, Health and Safety," *Police Quarterly* 5 (March 2002): 4-24; Vila, Bryan, and Dennis Jay Kenney, "Tired Cops: The Prevalence and Potential Consequences of Police Fatigue," *NIJ Journal* 248 (2002): 17-21, available at https://www.ncjrs.gov/pdffiles1/ jr000248d.pdf.

4. Rajaratnam, Shantha M.W., Laura K. Barger, Steven W. Lockley, Steven A. Shea, Wei Wang, Christopher P. Landrigan, Conor S. O'Brien, Salim Qadri, Jason P. Sullivan, Brian E. Cade, Lawrence J. Epstein, David P. White, and Charles A. Czeisler, "Sleep Disorders, Health, and Safety in Police Officers," *JAMA* 306 (2011): 2567-2578, available at http://jama.ama-assn.org/ content/306/23/2567.full.

5. Amendola, Karen L., David Weisburd, Edwin E. Hamilton, Greg Jones, and Meghan Slipka, *The Shift Length Experiment: What We Know About 8-, 10-, and 12-Hour Shifts in Policing,* Police Foundation, December 2011, available at http://www.policefoundation.org/ shiftexperiment.

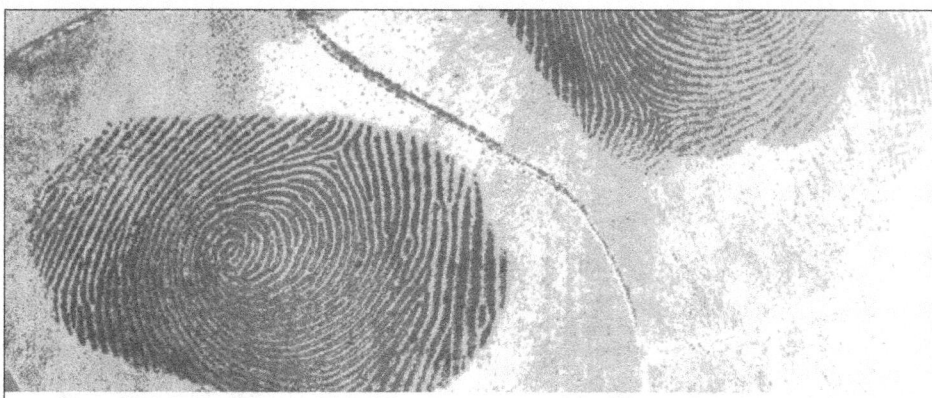

Improving Latent Fingerprint Examinations by Reducing Human Error

Fingerprint analysis is critical to the success of the nation's criminal justice system. In fact, fingerprints left at a crime scene — referred to as latent prints — are the most common type of forensic science evidence and have been used in criminal investigations for more than 100 years.

The examination of fingerprint evidence consists of a series of steps involving the comparison of a latent print to a known print ("exemplar"). During this step-by-step matching process, latent print examiners must reach correct conclusions; they are also expected to produce records of the examination and, in some cases, present their conclusions — and the reasoning behind them — in court.

In recent years, the accuracy of latent print identification has been the subject of increased study, scrutiny and commentary in the legal system and in forensic science literature. To help address this issue, NIJ and the U.S. National Institute of Standards and Technology convened an expert working group to do a scientific assessment of the effects of human factors on forensic latent print analysis and to develop recommendations to reduce the risk of error. Read the final report (http://nij.gov/pubs-sum/latent-print-human-factors.htm).

The panel addressed issues ranging from the acquisition of impressions of friction ridge skin to courtroom testimony, and from laboratory design and equipment to emerging methods for associating latent prints with exemplars. In addition to a comprehensive discussion of how human factors relate to all aspects of latent print examinations — including communicating conclusions through reports and testimony — the report offers important recommendations to improve the understanding and management of human-factor issues in fingerprint analysis.

One particularly helpful tool in the report is a flow chart of the Analysis, Comparison, Evaluation and Verification (ACE-V) process for latent-print examination, which is currently used in the nation's forensic crime laboratories. Developed by the working group, this flow chart (see page 41) is offered to facilitate discussion about key decision points in the ACE-V process, particularly regarding steps in the ACE-V process where human error risks could be minimized.

The Latent Print Examination Process Map
The Expert Working Group on Human Factors in Latent Print Analysis

Start

PRE-ANALYSIS ACTIVITY

- 10 Identify item relevant to the case that has potential for bearing latent prints
- 20 Physical item is documented and collected in the field for further analysis
- 30 The item is transmitted to the laboratory and chain of custody is documented
- 40 Latent print is developed/captured (applies to field or laboratory)
- 50 Is latent processing adequate?
- 60 Is the latent suitable for Analysis?
- 80 Latent print is retained as case evidence for further analysis
- 70 The latent print is deemed unsuitable and therefore is NOT preserved, collected or retained as case evidence for further analysis

ANALYSIS

- 100 Latent print enters the examination process
- 200 Latent print provided to latent print examiner for analysis
- 210 Analyze distinctive details of the latent print
- 220 Analyze relevant distortion in latent print
- 230 Analysis sufficient?
- 240 Suitable for comparison?
- 250 Determine appropriate (likely) orientation (up and down) and location (area of the skin) of the latent print
- 260 Known prints available?
- 270 Latent suitable for AFIS?
- 280 Latent is formatted, encoded and AFIS search performed
- 290 Determine and memorize a distinct target group of latent print detail to search
- 320 Analyze distinctive details of the known print
- 330 Analyze relevant distortion of the known print
- 340 Known print analysis adequate?
- 300 Known prints obtained by law enforcement agency & sent to laboratory
- 310 Known prints or candidates provided to the examiner for analysis
- 350 Known prints suitable for comparison?
- 360 Common area in latent and known prints?
- 370 Sufficient Quality and Quantity? (Suitable to compare?)
- 400 The latent is not compared but is retained as case evidence according to policy
- 410 Known prints obtained?

COMPARISON

- 500 Sufficient disagreement of Level 1 Detail?
- 530 Continue comparison of additional detail (levels 1, 2, & 3)
- 540 Dissimilarity present?
- 510 Target group exists within tolerance?
- 560 Similarity present?
- 520 Would new Target be beneficial?
- To 290

EVALUATION

- 600 Within tolerance for an ID?
- 620 Sufficient disagreement?
- 650 Sufficient agreement?
- 680 Reanalysis beneficial?
- To 210
- To 290
- 720 EXCLUSION
- 750 INDIVIDUALIZATION
- 780 INCONCLUSIVE

VERIFICATION

- 800 Refer to agency policy to determine if verification is required
- 810 Verification required?
- 820 Conclusion confirmed?
- 840 Conflict resolution according to organization policy
- 900 Results sent to requester

Stop

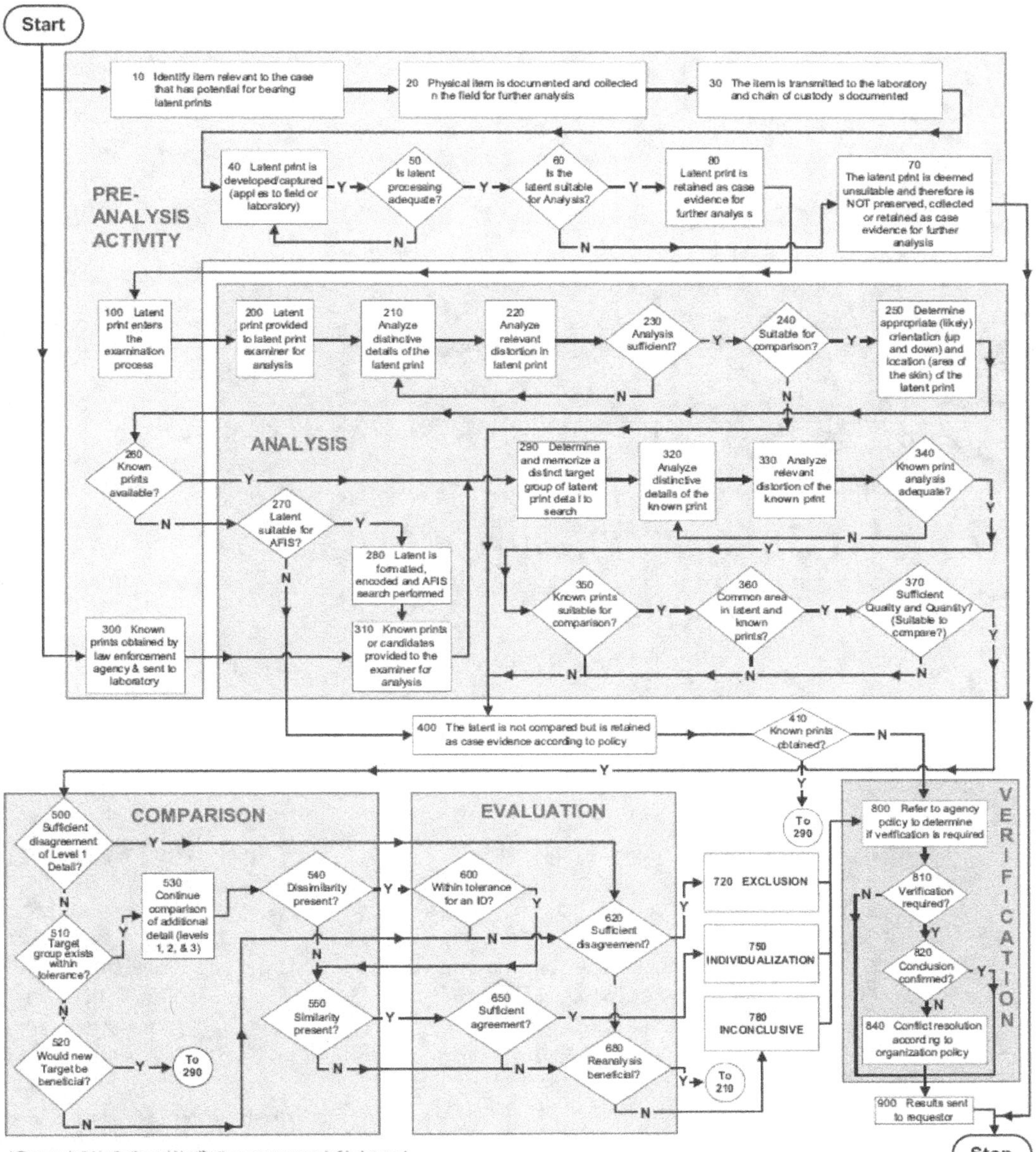

* The terms individualization and identification are synonymous in this document

To print out a larger version of this chart, go to http://nij.gov/nij/topics/forensics/evidence/impression/latent-print-flowchart.htm.

Legend: This diagram documents the steps of the ACE-V process as currently practiced by the latent print examination community. The numbers in each of the boxes correspond to "steps" that are more fully described in the report. The purpose of this process map is to facilitate discussion about key decision points in the ACE-V process.

Expert Working Group on Human Factors in Latent Print Analysis, *Latent Print Examination and Human Factors: Improving the Practice through a Systems Approach,* Washington, D.C.: U.S. Department of Commerce, National Institute of Standards and Technology, 2012

NIST
National Institute of Standards and Technology

OLES

NIJ
National Institute of Justice

http://www.nist.gov/oles/prints 022112 cfm

In Search of a Job: Criminal Records as Barriers to Employment

by Amy L. Solomon

Editor's note: Ms. Solomon co-chairs the staff working group of the Attorney General's Reentry Council. This article is an adaptation of her July 26, 2011, testimony before the Equal Employment Opportunity Commission.

" I am writing this letter … out of desperation and to tell you a little about the struggles of re-entering society as a convicted felon." Thus began a letter that made its way to me at the U.S. Department of Justice (DOJ). The letter came from a 30-year-old man who — in 2003, at age 21 — lost control of his car after a night of drinking, killing his close friend. "Jay" was convicted of involuntary manslaughter and sentenced to 38 months in state prison.

"I have worked hard to turn my life around. I have remained clean for nearly eight years, I am succeeding in college, and I continue to share my story in schools, treatment facilities and correctional institutions, yet I have nothing to show for it. … I have had numerous interviews and sent out more than 200 resumes for jobs which I am more than qualified. I have had denial after denial because of my felony." Jay ends the letter saying, "I do understand that you are not responsible for the choices that have brought me to this point. Furthermore, I recognize that if I was not abiding by the law, if I was not clean, and if I was not focusing my efforts toward a successful future, I would have no claim to make."

Jay's story is not unusual.

A Substantial Share of the U.S. Population Has Arrest Records

A new study shows that nearly one-third of American adults have been arrested by age 23.[1] This record will keep many people from obtaining employment, even if they have paid their dues, are qualified for the job and are unlikely to reoffend. At the same time, it is the chance at a job that offers hope for people involved in the criminal justice system, as we know from research that stable employment is an important predictor of successful re-entry and desistance from crime.[2]

Criminal records run the gamut — from one-time arrests where charges are dropped to lengthy, serious and violent criminal histories. Most arrests are for relatively minor or nonviolent offenses. Among the nearly 14 million arrests recorded in 2009, only 4 percent were considered among the most serious violent crimes (which include murder, rape, robbery and aggravated assault).[3] (See Figure 1.) Another 10 percent of all arrests were for simple assault; these do not involve a weapon or aggravated injury but often include domestic violence and intimate partner violence. The remainder of the arrests in 2009 were for:

■ Property crimes, which accounted for 18 percent of arrests. These include burglary, larceny-theft, motor vehicle theft, arson, vandalism, stolen property, forgery and counterfeiting, fraud, and embezzlement.

■ Drug offenses, which accounted for 12 percent of arrests. These include production, distribution and use of controlled substances.

■ Other offenses, which accounted for 56 percent of all arrests. These include disorderly conduct, drunkenness, prostitution, vagrancy, loitering, driving under the influence and weapons violations.

Although many of these "other" offenses are for behaviors that harm the community, they do not constitute the most serious violent offenses of murder, rape, robbery and aggravated assault.

Furthermore, what is often forgotten is that many people who have been arrested — and, therefore, technically have a criminal record that shows up on a background check — were never convicted of a crime. This is true not only among those charged with minor crimes, but also for many individuals arrested for serious offenses. A snapshot of felony filings in the 75 largest counties, for example, showed that approximately one-third of felony arrests did not lead to conviction.[4]

People of Color Are Disproportionately Impacted

The impact of having a criminal record is exacerbated among African Americans, who may already experience racial discrimination in the labor market and are more likely than whites to have a criminal record. Two prominent studies by Devah Pager involved employment audits of men in Milwaukee and New York City. Both studies, funded by NIJ, found that a criminal record reduces the likelihood of a job callback or offer by approximately 50 percent. This criminal record "penalty" was substantially greater for African Americans than for white applicants. The more recent study included Latinos in the test pool and showed they suffered similar "penalties" in the employment market.[5]

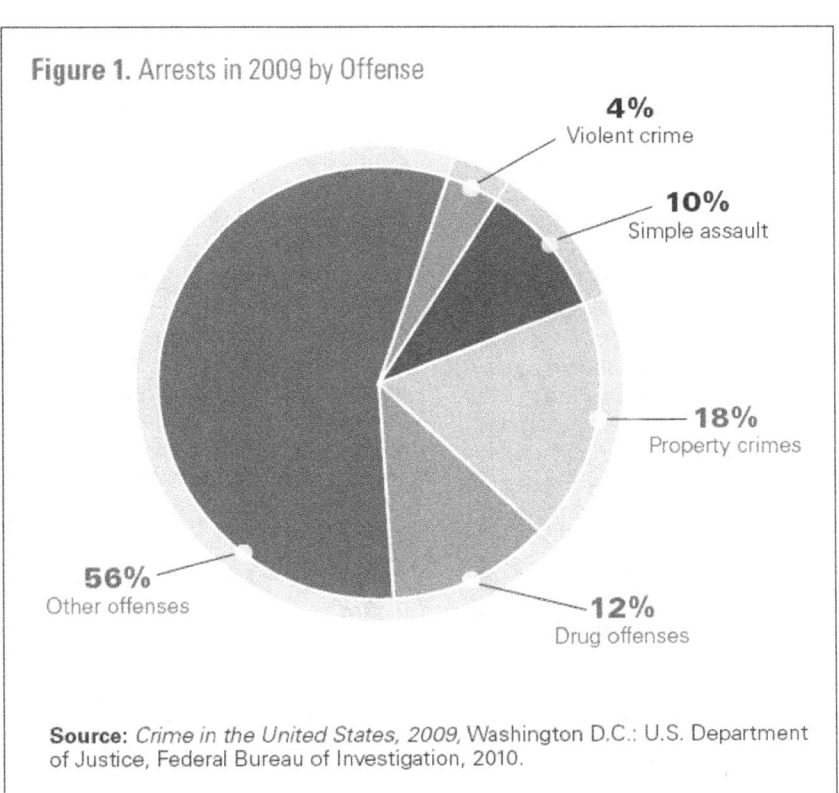

Figure 1. Arrests in 2009 by Offense

4% Violent crime

10% Simple assault

18% Property crimes

12% Drug offenses

56% Other offenses

Source: *Crime in the United States, 2009,* Washington D.C.: U.S. Department of Justice, Federal Bureau of Investigation, 2010.

Nearly 75 percent of arrestees are male. African Americans account for less than 14 percent of the U.S. population[6] but 28 percent of all arrests. They are even more highly represented in the incarcerated population, comprising almost 40 percent of those behind bars.[7]

Although many arrests do not lead to conviction, and many convictions do not result in imprisonment, the incarcerated population is substantial. Each year, there are almost 13 million people admitted to — and released from — local jails[8] and more than 700,000 admitted to/released from state and federal prisons.[9] Incarceration rates in the United States are higher than in any other country in the world. The United States has less than 5 percent of the world's population but almost a quarter of the world's prisoners.[10] Over the last 30 years, the incarcerated population has more than quadrupled, and today, just under 2.3 million men and women are held in prisons and jails.[11]

In 2008, the Pew Center on the States brought heightened public attention to our nation's incarceration rate when it reported that 1 in 100 U.S. adults was behind bars on any given day.[12] (See Figure 2.) One in 100 is substantial, but it is also an average that does not hold evenly across all populations. One in 54 men is incarcerated, compared to 1 in 265 women. Looking just at men, we see that 1 in 106 white men is behind bars, compared to 1 in 36 Hispanic men and 1 in 15 African American men. When we consider young African American men (ages 20-34), the ratio lowers further to 1 in 9. In fact, young, male African American high school dropouts have higher odds of being in jail than being employed.[13] As these numbers make clear, incarceration is heavily concentrated among men, particularly young men of color.

There is also an intergenerational component at work. Forty-six percent of jail inmates have a family member who was incarcerated.[14] On any given day, 1 in 28 children has a parent behind bars. Again, communities of color are most acutely affected; 1 in 9 African American children has an incarcerated parent.[15] One recent study estimates that 25

> The majority of employers indicate that they would "probably" or "definitely" not be willing to hire an applicant with a criminal record.

percent of African Americans born after 1990 will witness their father being sent to prison before their 14th birthday.[16]

Incarceration is also a geographically concentrated phenomenon. A large number of prisoners come from — and return to — a relatively small number of already disadvantaged neighborhoods.[17] In many neighborhoods around the country, incarceration is no longer an unusual occurrence but a commonplace experience, especially for young men of color.

Incarcerated Populations Face a Broad Set of Challenges

The corrections population consists largely of men who have for many years exhibited a consistent pattern of criminal involvement, a lack of attachment to mainstream institutions of social integration and a

multiplicity of interconnected problems. Among jail inmates:

- Sixty-eight percent meet the criteria for substance abuse or dependence.[18]

- Sixty percent do not have a high school diploma or general equivalency diploma.[19]

- Thirty percent were unemployed in the month before arrest, and almost twice as many were underemployed.[20]

- Sixteen percent are estimated to have serious mental health problems.[21]

- Fourteen percent were homeless at some point during the year before they were incarcerated.[22]

The need for treatment, training and assistance is great.[23] It is critical that individuals entering prisons and jails be screened and assessed to determine their criminogenic risks and needs, and that appropriate evidence-based interventions be applied during incarceration and after release to produce the best outcomes.[24]

Collateral Consequences Create Additional Barriers

In addition to these significant and often overlapping challenges, an extra set of punishments, or "collateral consequences," is imposed on individuals as a direct result of their criminal convictions. NIJ is funding a national study, conducted by the American Bar Association's Criminal Justice Section, which has catalogued more than 38,000 statutes that impose collateral consequences on people convicted of crimes, creating barriers to jobs, housing, benefits and voting.[25] More than 80 percent of the statutes operate as a denial of employment opportunities.

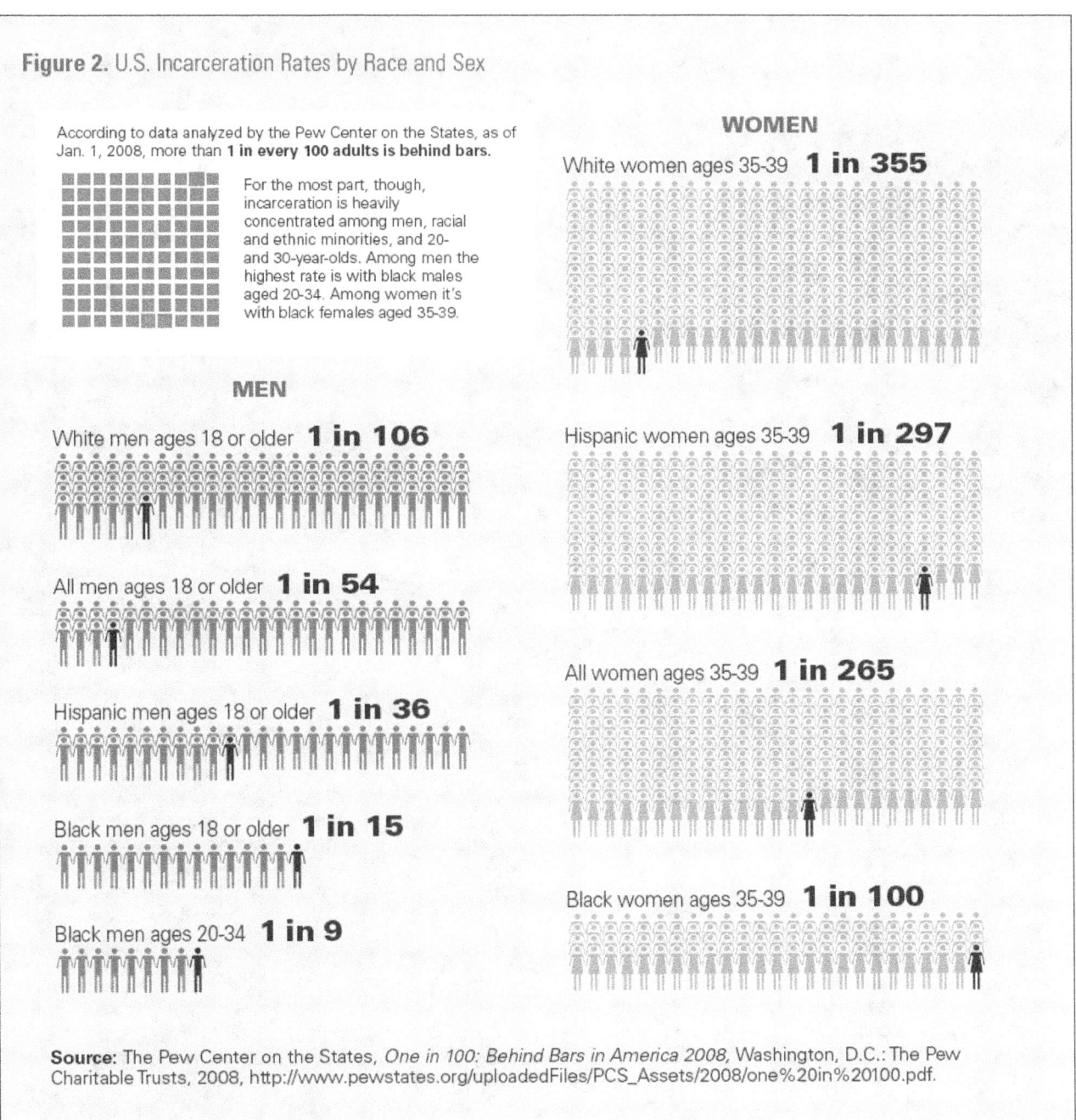

Figure 2. U.S. Incarceration Rates by Race and Sex

According to data analyzed by the Pew Center on the States, as of Jan. 1, 2008, more than **1 in every 100 adults is behind bars.**

For the most part, though, incarceration is heavily concentrated among men, racial and ethnic minorities, and 20- and 30-year-olds. Among men the highest rate is with black males aged 20-34. Among women it's with black females aged 35-39.

WOMEN

White women ages 35-39 **1 in 355**

Hispanic women ages 35-39 **1 in 297**

All women ages 35-39 **1 in 265**

Black women ages 35-39 **1 in 100**

MEN

White men ages 18 or older **1 in 106**

All men ages 18 or older **1 in 54**

Hispanic men ages 18 or older **1 in 36**

Black men ages 18 or older **1 in 15**

Black men ages 20-34 **1 in 9**

Source: The Pew Center on the States, *One in 100: Behind Bars in America 2008*, Washington, D.C.: The Pew Charitable Trusts, 2008, http://www.pewstates.org/uploadedFiles/PCS_Assets/2008/one%20in%20100.pdf.

Although some of these consequences serve important public safety purposes, others may be antiquated and create unnecessary barriers to legitimate work opportunities. A commonly cited example is that in some states, formerly incarcerated people who were trained as barbers cannot hold those jobs after release because state laws prohibit felons from practicing the trade, presumably because their access to sharp objects makes them a threat to the public.[26]

U.S. Attorney General Eric Holder recently wrote to every state Attorney General, with a copy to

The Attorney General's Reentry Council

In January 2011, U.S. Attorney General Eric Holder established a Cabinet-level federal interagency Reentry Council, representing a significant executive branch commitment to coordinating re-entry efforts and advancing effective re-entry policies. The Reentry Council is premised on a real recognition that many federal agencies — not just the Department of Justice (DOJ) — have a major stake in re-entry. The re-entry population is one with which we are all already working — not only in prisons, jails and juvenile facilities, but in emergency rooms, homeless shelters, unemployment lines, child support offices, veterans hospitals and elsewhere. When we extend out to the children and families of returning prisoners, the intersection is even greater.

At its first meeting, the council adopted a mission statement to advance public safety and well-being through enhanced communication, coordination and collaboration across federal agency initiatives that: (1) make communities safer by reducing recidivism and victimization, (2) assist those who return from prison and jail in becoming productive citizens, and (3) save taxpayer dollars by lowering the direct and collateral costs of incarceration. The council has empowered staff — now representing 20 federal departments and agencies — to work toward a number of goals organized around coordinating and leveraging federal resources for re-entry; removing federal barriers to re-entry; and using the bully pulpit to dispel myths, educating key stakeholders about federal policies, resources and effective reentry models.

Regarding employment and re-entry, the council has an active working group composed of staff from the Department of Labor (DOL), DOJ, the Office of Personnel Management, the Equal Employment Opportunity Commission (EEOC), the Federal Trade Commission and the Small Business Administration, among others. The council has developed public education materials, a website and a set of "Reentry MythBusters" to clarify federal policy on a number of issues. Five MythBusters focus on employer responsibilities and incentives as well as worker rights in this area. On the incentives side, DOL offers both tax credits and federal bonding protection for employers that hire ex-offenders. On the employer-responsibility and worker rights side, an EEOC-authored MythBuster provides guidance to employers about the appropriate use of a criminal record in making hiring decisions.[1]

The EEOC has long-standing guidance on this issue and is doing enhanced, extensive training and outreach. In July 2011, the Commission held a meeting focused exclusively on arrest and conviction records as barriers to employment. After substantial consideration and review of the information presented both at

every Governor, asking them to assess their state's collateral consequences and determine if any should be eliminated "so that people who have paid their debt to society are able to live and work productively."[27] The Attorney General's letter also said the federal government would assess the federal collateral consequences — and through the auspices of the interagency Reentry Council, we are doing just that.

Regardless of the legal restrictions, the majority of employers indicate that they would "probably" or "definitely" not be willing to hire an applicant with a criminal record, according to a study by Harry Holzer and colleagues.[28] In fact, a recent report by the National Employment Law Project found frequent use of blanket "no-hire" policies among major corporations, as evidenced by their online job ads posted on Craigslist.[29]

The employer motivation is understandable. Employers do not want to hire individuals who might commit future crimes and who may be a risk to their employees' and customers' safety. The assumption, of course, is that a prior record signals higher odds that the individual will commit more crimes in the future. A key question is: If a person who has been arrested stays *arrest-free* for some period of time, do the odds of further criminal the meeting and during the public comment period, the EEOC voted 4-1 to issue updated enforcement guidance. The revised guidance, issued April 25, 2012, calls for employers to assess applicants on an individual basis rather than excluding everyone with a criminal record through a blanket policy. It provides new detail and direction for employers in how to consider three key factors — the nature of the job; the nature and seriousness of the offense; and the length of time since it occurred — in writing a hiring policy and in making a specific hiring decision. The updated guidance also emphasizes that employers should not reject a candidate because of an arrest without a conviction, as arrests are not proof of criminal conduct. "The ability of African-Americans and Hispanics to gain employment after prison is one of the paramount civil justice issues of our time," said Commissioner Stuart J. Ishimaru in his statement at the April 25 meeting.

Additionally, in January 2012, the EEOC announced an important settlement agreement with Pepsi regarding its use of arrest and conviction records in employment.[2] The company's policy excluded applicants arrested for any crime — even if they had never been convicted of any offense — from permanent employment. The EEOC found that the criminal background check policy discriminated against African Americans in violation of Title VII of the Civil Rights Act of 1964. This was the first public conciliation concerning the use of arrest and conviction records and is already raising awareness among employers. During fiscal year 2010 and fiscal year 2011, the Commission received more than 1,200 charges alleging job discrimination involving criminal background checks.

DOL is also playing a critical role in this area. In addition to substantial investments in re-entry programs and research, DOL is making important commitments to educate its broad network of employment and training entities on these issues. In June 2010, Secretary Hilda L. Solis hosted a roundtable on workforce development and employment strategies for people with criminal records, and she has gone on record with strong statements on the topic. As she stated at the June roundtable, "When someone serves time in our penal system, they shouldn't face a lifetime sentence of unemployment when they are released. Those who want to make amends must be given the opportunity to make an honest living."[3]

Notes

1. Reentry MythBusters and additional information about the Reentry Council are available at http://www.nationalreentryresourcecenter.org/reentry-council.

2. See Equal Employment Opportunity Commission, "Pepsi to Pay $3.13 Million and Made Major Policy Changes to Resolve EEOC Finding of Nationwide Hiring Discrimination Against African Americans," press release, January 11, 2012, http://www.eeoc.gov/eeoc/newsroom/release/1-11-12a.cfm; and Hananel, Sam, "Pepsi Beverages Pays $3M in Racial Bias Case," *USA Today* (January 11, 2012), http://www.usatoday.com/money/industries/food/story/2012-01-11/pepsi-racial-bias-case/52498132/1.

3. Remarks of Hilda L. Solis, Secretary of Labor, "Workforce Development and Employment Strategies for the Formerly-Incarcerated," June 21, 2011, https://www.dol.gov/_sec/media/speeches/20110621_EX.htm.

activity go down? A recent study sheds light on just this issue.

Alfred Blumstein and Kiminori Nakamura conducted the NIJ-funded "Redemption Study." They were looking for a way to empirically determine when it is no longer necessary for an employer to be concerned about a criminal record in a prospective employee's past.[30] The researchers examined the criminal records of everyone who was arrested for the first time in 1980 in the state of New York. They then tracked those criminal records forward to find who was arrested again, who wasn't and how long people "stayed clean." In general, once a person had stayed clean for a certain period of time, his chances of being arrested for a new crime were substantially reducedThis is what the researchers refer to as the "point of redemption" — when a prior arrest no longer distinguishes that person from a similar person in the general population in terms of the risk of future criminal arrests.

For individuals who commit their first crime at a very young age or who are first arrested for a more serious crime, it takes longer — about eight years — to reach the point of redemption; but for those who are older when first arrested or who commit less serious crimes, the point of redemption can come in as little as three or four years. After staying clean for this period of time, these individuals become indistinguishable from the general population in terms of their odds of another arrest.[31]

This research has important practical implications. Blumstein and Nakamura suggest that "forever rules be replaced by rules that provide for the expiration of a criminal record." They continue, in an op-ed published by *The New York Times,* that "it is unreasonable for someone to be hounded by a single arrest or conviction that happened more than 20 years earlier — and for many kinds of crimes, the records should be sealed even sooner."[32]

Some states are taking steps in exactly this direction.[33] Thirteen states enacted laws in their 2010-2011 legislative sessions to expunge and seal low-level offenses after a discrete number of years. Three states passed laws to limit the liability of employers that hire people with criminal records.[34]

This is not to say that criminal background checks serve no purpose. They give employers a tool — albeit an imperfect one — for helping assess risk to their employees, customers, assets and reputations when making hiring decisions. In fact, some of the same research cited earlier indicates that the use of criminal history records and the practice of performing background checks can, in some cases, *reduce* racial discrimination in hiring. The Holzer study, in particular, suggests that employers that perform background checks may end up hiring more African American workers (especially African American men) than those that do not perform

them. This is because some employers may assume young African American men have criminal records, and a background check may actually dispel that assumption and increase their chances of being hired.

> If a person who has been arrested stays *arrest-free* for some period of time, do the odds of further criminal activity go down?

It is also important to note that criminal records are often incomplete and inaccurate. A DOJ report states that "no single source exists that provides complete and up-to-date information about a person's criminal history."[35] Even the best-maintained record systems are incomplete, often lacking final disposition information in 50 percent or more of the records.[36] If criminal records were a perfect reflection of a person's criminal history, the need for this discussion would be less critical.

Focusing on Prisoner Re-Entry

As noted earlier, incarceration rates are high, and nearly everyone in prison will eventually be released. When re-entry fails, the costs — both societal and economic — are high. More than two-thirds of state prisoners are rearrested within three years of their release, and half are reincarcerated.[37] High rates of

recidivism mean more crime, more victims and more pressure on federal, state and municipal budgets. In the past 20 years, state spending on corrections has grown at a faster rate than nearly any other state budget item. The United States now spends more than $74 billion annually on federal, state and local corrections.[38]

The good news is that the response being mounted to meet these challenges is robust. Because re-entry intersects with issues such as health, housing, education, employment, family, faith and community well-being, many federal agencies are focusing on the re-entry population with initiatives that aim to improve outcomes in each of these areas (see sidebar, "The Attorney General's Reentry Council"). Congress has supported re-entry efforts as well. The Second Chance Act was passed by Congress with strong bipartisan support and then signed into law by President Bush in 2008. Senators Patrick Leahy (D-VT) and Rob Portman (R-OH) introduced S. 1231, the Second Chance Reauthorization Act of 2011. Re-entry efforts are under way all over the country, and strong bipartisan support is found in state houses and city halls, on county commissions, and in community forums.

Moving Forward

These issues are large-scale and impact an increasingly sizable share of our population. In some distressed communities, arrest and incarceration are commonplace occurrences and part of daily life. Getting a job is arguably the most important step toward successful re-entry for people who have broken the law and paid their debt to society. Yet too many people are barred from job opportunities and thus denied a critical chance to succeed.

Guidance to Employers and Job Seekers on the Use of Criminal Records in the Hiring Process

A 2010 survey by the Society for Human Resource Management reported that 92 percent of employers conduct background checks on job applicants. According to the Equal Employment Opportunity Commission (EEOC), if an employer is aware of a conviction or incarceration, that information should bar someone from employment only when the conviction is closely related to the job, after considering: (1) the nature of the job, (2) the nature and seriousness of the offense, and (3) the length of time since it occurred. Because an arrest alone does not necessarily mean that someone has committed a crime, an employer should allow the person to explain the circumstances of the arrest and again assess whether the circumstances of the arrest are closely related to the job. In the vast majority of cases, employers may not automatically bar everyone with an arrest or conviction record from employment because it could have a disparate impact on communities of color, violating

Title VII of the Civil Rights Act of 1964. The EEOC's guidance in this area was revised in April 2012. It now provides greater detail and direction to employers on the appropriate use of arrest and conviction records in hiring decisions.

It is important that job applicants know their rights. The Fair Credit Reporting Act (FCRA) requires employers to receive an applicant's permission, usually in writing, before asking a background screening company for a criminal history report. If the applicant does not give permission, the application for employment may not get reviewed. If a person does give permission but does not get hired because of information in the report, the potential employer has several legal obligations. Specifically, they must tell the individual:

■ The name, address and telephone number of the company that supplied the criminal history report

■ That the company that supplied the criminal history information did not make the decision to take the

adverse action and cannot give specific reasons for it

■ About his or her right to dispute the accuracy or completeness of any information in the report, and his or her right to an additional free report from the company that supplied the criminal history report, if requested within 60 days of the adverse action

For more information:

■ Reentry MythBusters on the EEOC guidance: http://www. nationalreentryresourcecenter. org/documents/0000/1082/ Reentry_Council_Mythbuster_ Employment.pdf

■ FCRA and criminal background checks: http://www. nationalreentryresourcecenter. org/documents/0000/1176/ Reentry_Council_Mythbuster_ FCRA_Employment.pdf

■ Revised EEOC guidance, issued April 25, 2012: http://www.eeoc. gov/laws/guidance/arrest_ conviction.cfm

The argument here is not about giving preference to this population when it comes to jobs. And employers certainly have a right to consider a person's criminal history in making a hiring decision. The concern is that some employers cast an overly broad net banning this population altogether. What is important is that people have an opportunity to apply and be considered for jobs when they are qualified and when their criminal record is not relevant or occurred long enough in the past

to no longer be a significant factor in predicting future behavior.

In following up with Jay, I learned that he now has two part-time jobs at local broadcasting companies. He holds himself accountable for his crime, but is also encouraged that he can make positive contributions and is eager to help others. It is critical that we, as a society, provide a path for individuals who have served their time and paid their debts to compete for legitimate work opportunities.

It is, in fact, our only choice if we want people with past criminal involvement to be able to support themselves and their families, pay their taxes, and contribute to our communities.

About the author: Amy L. Solomon is a Senior Advisor to the Assistant Attorney General in the Office of Justice Programs at the U.S. Department of Justice.

NCJ 238488

For more information:

■ Learn more about Devah Pager's research on the impact of conviction status on the employment prospects of young men at http://www.nij.gov/topics/corrections/reentry/employment.htm.

■ Read "'Redemption' in an Era of Widespread Criminal Background Checks," by Alfred Blumstein and Kiminori Nakamura, at http://www.nij.gov/journals/263/redemption.htm.

Watch Alfred Blumstein and Kiminori Nakamura discuss how their research findings could have implications for hiring decisions: http://nij.ncjrs.gov/multimedia/video-nijconf2009-blumstein-nakamura.htm.

Read the Reentry MythBusters: http://www.nationalreentryresourcecenter.org/documents/0000/1090/REENTRY_MYTHBUSTERS.pdf.

Learn more at the Reentry Council's website, http://www.nationalreentryresourcecenter.org/reentry-council.

Notes

1. Barnes, Robert, Michael G. Turner, Raymond Paternoster, and Shawn D. Bushway, "Cumulative Prevalence of Arrest From Ages 8 to 23 in a National Sample," *Pediatrics* (January 2012): 21-27, http://pediatrics.aappublications.org/content/129/1/21.abstract.

2. Visher, Christy A., Laura Winterfield, and Mark B. Coggeshall, "Ex-Offender Employment Programs and Recidivism: A Meta-Analysis," *Journal of Experimental Criminology* 1 (2005): 295-316. See also Laub, John H., and Robert J. Sampson, "Understanding Desistance from Crime," *Crime & Justice* 28(1): 17-24, http://www.wjh.harvard.edu/soc/faculty/sampson/articles/2001_C&J_Laub.pdf.

3. *Crime in the United States, 2009,* Washington, D.C.: U.S. Department of Justice, Federal Bureau of Investigation, 2010, http://www2.fbi.gov/ucr/cius2009/index.html.

4. Cohen, Thomas H., and Tracey Kyckelhahn, *Felony Defendants in Large Urban Counties, 2006,* Bulletin, Washington, D.C.: U.S. Department of Justice, Bureau of Justice Statistics, 2010, NCJ 228944, http://bjs.ojp.usdoj.gov/content/pub/pdf/fdluc06.pdf.

5. Pager, Devah, "The Mark of a Criminal Record," *American Journal of Sociology* 108 (2003): 957-960, http://www.princeton.edu/~pager/pager_ajs.pdf; Pager, Devah, Bruce Western, and Bart Bonikowski, "Discrimination in a Low-Wage Labor Market: A Field Experiment," *American Sociological Review* 74 (October 2009): 777-779, http://www.princeton.edu/~pager/ASR_pager_etal09.pdf.

6. Rastogi, Sonya, Tallese D. Johnson, Elizabeth M. Hoeffel, and Malcolm P. Drewery, Jr., *The Black Population: 2010,* 2010 Census Briefs, Washington, D.C.: U.S. Department of Commerce, U.S. Census Bureau, 2011, http://www.census.gov/prod/cen2010/briefs/c2010br-06.pdf.

7. Sabol, William J., Todd D. Minton, and Paige M. Harrison, *Prison and Jail Inmates at Midyear 2006,* Bulletin, Washington, D.C.: U.S. Department of Justice, Bureau of Justice Statistics, 2011, NCJ 217675, http://bjs.ojp.usdoj.gov/content/pub/pdf/pjim06.pdf.

8. Minton, Todd D., *Jail Inmates at Midyear 2010,* Statistical Tables, Washington, D.C.: U.S. Department of Justice, Bureau of Justice Statistics, April 2011, NCJ 233431, http://bjs.ojp.usdoj.gov/content/pub/pdf/jim10st.pdf.

9. Guerino, Paul, Paige M. Harrison, and William J. Sabol, *Prisoners in 2010,* Bulletin, Washington, D.C.: U.S. Department of Justice, Bureau of Justice Statistics, December 2011, NCJ 236096, http://bjs.ojp.usdoj.gov/content/pub/pdf/p10.pdf.

10. Walmsley, Roy, *World Prison Population List,* 8th ed., London: King's College, 2008.

11. Glaze, Laura, *Correctional Population in the United States, 2010,* Bulletin, Washington, D.C.: U.S. Department of Justice, Bureau of Justice Statistics, December 2011, NCJ 236319, http://www.bjs.gov/content/pub/pdf/cpus10.pdf.

12. The Pew Center on the States, *One in 100: Behind Bars in America 2008,* Washington, D.C.: The Pew Charitable Trusts, 2008, http://www.pewstates.org/uploadedFiles/PCS_Assets/2008/one%20in%20100.pdf.

13. The Pew Charitable Trusts, *Collateral Costs: Incarceration's Effect on Economic Mobility,* Washington, D.C.: The Pew Charitable Trusts, 2010, http://www.pewstates.org/uploaded-Files/PCS_Assets/2010/Collateral_Costs(1).pdf.

14. James, Doris J., *Profile of Jail Inmates, 2002,* Special Report, Washington, D.C.: U.S. Department of Justice, Bureau of Justice Statistics, 2004, NCJ 201932, http://bjs.ojp.usdoj.gov/content/pub/pdf/pji02.pdf.

15. The Pew Charitable Trusts, *Collateral Costs: Incarceration's Effect on Economic Mobility.*

16. Western, Bruce, "Reentry: Reversing Mass Imprisonment," *Boston Review* (July/August 2008), http://www.bostonreview.net/BR33.4/western.php.

17. Visher, Christy A., Jennifer Yahner, and Nancy LaVigne, "Life After Prison: Tracking the Experiences of Male Prisoners Returning to Chicago, Cleveland, and Houston,"

Washington, D.C.: Urban Institute, 2010; Cadora, Eric, "Criminal Justice and Health and Human Services: An Exploration of Overlapping Needs, Resources, and Interests in Brooklyn Neighborhoods," Washington, D.C.: Urban Institute, 2002.

18. Karberg, Jennifer, and Doris James, *Substance Dependence, Abuse, and Treatment of Jail Inmates, 2002,* Special Report, Washington, D.C.: U.S. Department of Justice, Bureau of Justice Statistics, 2005, NCJ 209588, http://bjs.ojp.usdoj.gov/content/pub/pdf/sdatji02.pdf.

19. Harlow, Caroline Wolf, *Education and Correctional Populations,* Special Report, Washington, D.C.: U.S. Department of Justice, Bureau of Justice Statistics, 2003, NCJ 195670.

20. James, Doris J., *Profile of Jail Inmate, 2002,* Special Report, Washington D.C.: U.S. Department of Justice, Bureau of Justice Statistics, 2004, NCJ 201932, http://bjs.ojp.usdoj.gov/content/pub/pdf/pji02.pdf.

21. Ditton, Paula, *Mental Health and Treatment of Inmates and Probationers,* Special Report, Washington, D.C.: U.S. Department of Justice, Bureau of Justice Statistics, 1999, NCJ 174463.

22. James, Doris J., *Profile of Jail Inmates, 2002.*

23. Federal Interagency Reentry Council, *Reentry in Brief: A Product of the Federal Interagency Reentry Council,* May 2011, http://www.nationalreentryresourcecenter.org/documents/0000/1059/Reentry_Brief.pdf.

24. For a more thorough discussion of the challenges facing the incarcerated population and re-entry models to address these challenges, see Solomon, Amy L., Jenny W.L. Osborne, Stefan F. LoBuglio, Jeff Mellow, and Debbie A. Mukamal, *Life After Lockup: Improving Reentry From Jail to the Community,* Washington, D.C.: Urban Institute, 2008, http://www.urban.org/UploadedPDF/411660_life_after_lockup.pdf.

25. Available at: American Bar Association, "Adult Collateral Consequences Project," July 2011, http://isrweb.isr.temple.

edu/projects/accproject. See also, Blumstein, Alfred, and Kiminori Nakamura, "'Redemption' in an Era of Widespread Criminal Background Checks," *NIJ Journal* 263 (June 2009): 10-17, http://www.nij.gov/journals/263/redemption.htm.

26. Haberman, Clyde, "Ex-Inmate's Legacy: Victory Over Bias and Catch-22 Bureaucracy," *New York Times* 29 (August 2008): B5.

27. Holder, Eric H., Jr., Letter, April 18, 2011, National Reentry Resource Center, http://www.nationalreentryresourcecenter.org/documents/0000/1088/Reentry_Council_AG_Letter.pdf.

28. Holzer, Harry J., Steven Raphael, and Michael A. Stoll, "Perceived Criminality, Criminal Background Checks, and the Racial Hiring Practices of Employers," *The Journal of Law and Economics* 49 (2006): 451, 453-454.

29. Rodriguez, Michelle N., and Maurice Emsellem, *65 Million 'Need Not Apply': The Case for Reforming Criminal Background Checks for Employment,* New York: National Employment Law Project, March 2011.

30. Blumstein, Alfred, and Kiminori Nakamura, "'Redemption' in an Era of Widespread Criminal Background Checks," *NIJ Journal* 263 (June 2009): 10-17, http://www.nij.gov/journals/263/redemption.htm. It is worth emphasizing that this research was based on first-time arrests, and the subjects were rarely incarcerated or were incarcerated for short periods of time. First-time arrestees rarely go to prison. Blumstein and Nakamura were recently awarded a new grant to examine "redemption" times for re-entering prisoners.

31. To test the general applicability of their results, Blumstein and Nakamura have conducted additional research in two other states and with two other sampling years. Their results are consistent, especially after the first five years after initial arrest. NIJ is currently funding Blumstein and Nakamura to test the robustness of the previous findings and to look at out-of-state arrests and racial differences.

32. Blumstein, Alfred, and Kiminori Nakamura, "Paying a Price, Long

After the Crime," *New York Times* (January 9, 2012), http://www.nytimes.com/2012/01/10/opinion/paying-a-price-long-after-the-crime.html?_r=2&ref=opinion.

33. National Employment Law Project, *State Reforms Promoting Employment of People With Criminal Records: 2010-11 Legislative Round-Up,* Legislative Update, December 2011, http://www.nelp.org/page/-/SCLP/2011/PromotingEmploymentofPeoplewithCriminalRecords.pdf?nocdn=1.

34. Ibid.

35. U.S. Department of Justice, Office of the Attorney General, *The Attorney General's Report on Criminal History Background Checks,* Washington, D.C.: U.S. Department of Justice, Office of the Attorney General, June 2006, http://www.justice.gov/olp/ag_bgchecks_report.pdf. The report states that approximately 50 percent of the records in the FBI's criminal history record repository are missing final disposition information. More recent arrest records, however, have a higher rate of completeness.

36. Also note that even after a criminal record has been expunged, the record can still appear in private database searches. See SEARCH Group, *Report of the National Task Force on the Commercial Sale of Criminal Justice Record Information,* SEARCH Group: Sacramento, Calif., 2005, http://www.search.org/files/pdf/RNTFCSCJRI.pdf.

37. Beck, A.J., "The Importance of Successful Reentry to Jail Population Growth," presented at the Urban Institute's Jail Re-Entry Roundtable, Washington, D.C., June 27, 2006, http://www.urban.org/projects/reentry-roundtable/upload/beck.PPT.

38. Bureau of Justice Statistics, "BJS Expenditure and Employment Data Collections," Washington, D.C.: U.S. Department of Justice, Bureau of Justice Statistics, http://bjs.ojp.usdoj.gov/index.cfm?ty=tp&tid=5; Kyckelhahn, Tracey, *Justice Expenditures and Employment, FY 1982-2007,* Statistical Tables, Washington, D.C.: U.S. Department of Justice, Bureau of Justice Statistics, December 2011, NCJ 236218, http://www.bjs.gov/content/pub/pdf/jee8207st.pdf.

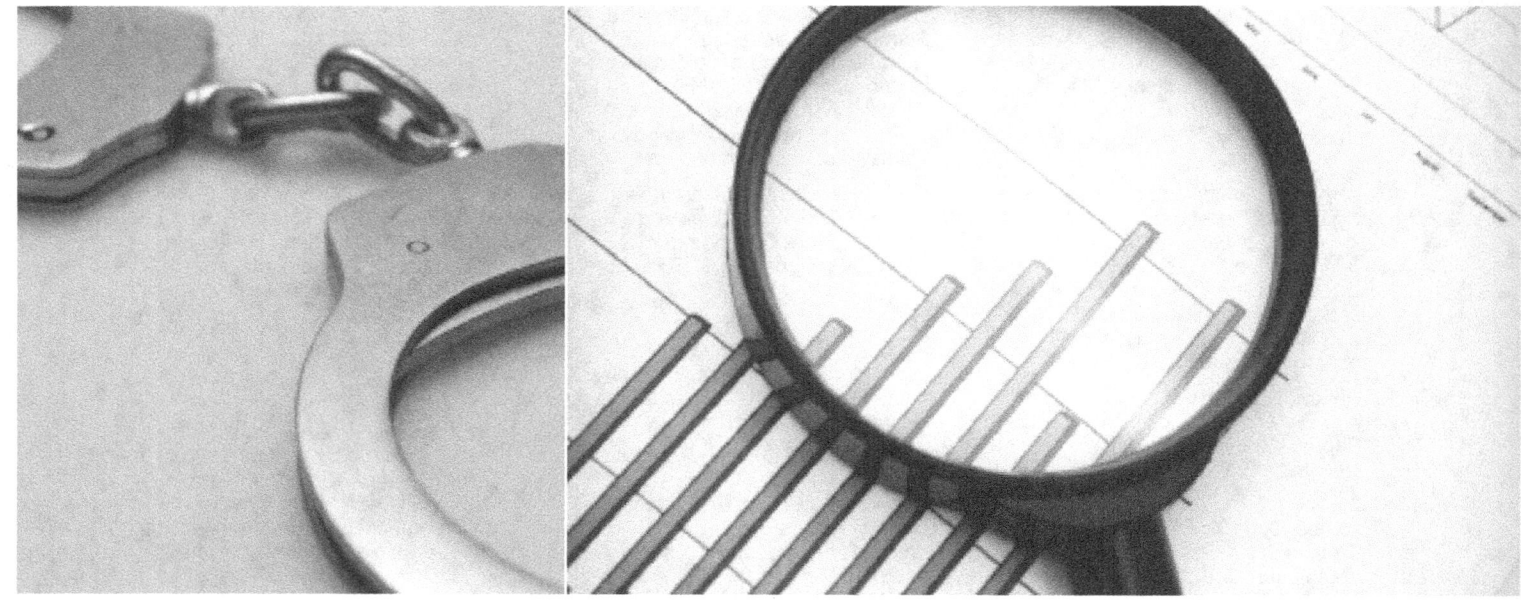

The Economist's Guide to Crime Busting

by Philip J. Cook and Jens Ludwig

The old divide between hard and soft strategies is breaking down under a wave of new thinking about how to control crime.

What is the more cost-effective way to control crime? Is it to focus on making crime unattractive by threatening offenders with long prison terms? Or to make the law-abiding life more attractive by providing better education and job opportunities? It's an old debate. The federal crime commissions of the 1960s emphasized crime's links with poverty and racism, and President Lyndon B. Johnson's Great Society programs were central to his war on crime. But ultimately the "hawks" won the debate about how to wage that war, as they did later in helping to launch President Richard M. Nixon's war on drugs. The result has been plain to see, with the rate of imprisonment surging to unprecedented heights.

Now the debate has been reopened. It is not so much that the public views mass incarceration, with its disproportionately high levels of imprisonment for blacks and Hispanics, as immoral or racist. Rather, the dreary fact is that, in the face of gaping budget deficits, the states can no longer afford to support huge prison populations. It seems like a good time for the economists to weigh in, in part because their perspective provides a way to get past the stale debates over whether to adopt "tough" or "soft" solutions.

The economic theory of crime starts with the premise that crime is a choice. It is not the result of character or culture, or not only of

those things, but is at bottom a product of decisions individuals make in response to their available options. Most of us choose to abstain from crime in part because we have a lot to lose if we get caught. Even so, we may slip up occasionally — say, at tax time or when driving — but generally the temptations of crime are not strong enough to override our restraint. The calculus for an unemployed dropout with readily available criminal options and few licit prospects is likely to appear quite different.

This economic perspective generates a nicely symmetrical approach to crime control. Crime policy should focus both on making criminal opportunities less tempting and on making the law-abiding life more rewarding. We can debate how best to accomplish each of those aims (and long prison terms are by no means the only answer for reducing temptation), but it's important to realize that they are closely linked: The threat of arrest and imprisonment is sharper for those who have something to lose, so giving at-risk people a bigger stake in the law-abiding life is a deterrent to crime.

Of course, this logic doesn't always work out. One reason so many people were shocked by the criminal charges against NFL stars Michael Vick (for staging dog fights) and Plaxico Burress (for carrying a gun illegally) is that both had so much to lose. But these cases help prove the rule precisely because they are so rare. When high-income people commit serious crimes, it is much more often in response to opportunities for great financial gain: Investment bilker Bernard Madoff comes to mind, along with Enron president Jeffrey Skilling and publishing magnate Conrad Black. Thankfully, most of

us are spared the temptation to rake in millions from fraudulent dealings by the simple fact that we wouldn't even know how to begin.

The "crime as choice" perspective expands the discussion of crime control from the question of how many new prisons we need to a wider-ranging consideration of how to make illicit choices less attractive.

> The economic theory of crime starts with the premise that crime is a choice.

Here we will focus on three proposals: raising the minimum age at which youths can leave school, promoting business improvement districts and other forms of self-protection, and increasing taxes on alcohol. To understand why these measures' moment has arrived, it's first necessary to take a brief excursion into the recent history of American crime control efforts.

The most notable feature of that history is that the rate of incarceration has increased by a factor of seven in the last generation. America now locks up 1 percent of its adult population — the highest rate of imprisonment in the world. While many thoughtful people are uneasy about our policy of mass incarceration, a good number believe that it is justified by the dramatic reductions in crime since the early 1990s. Homicide and robbery rates have declined to levels not seen since the early 1960s. Property crime rates have fallen even more dramatically. As a result, America's cities have

seen big improvements in property values and the quality of life. Harlem and many other urban communities that were once hobbled by pervasive crime are thriving. Washington, D.C., the murder capital of the country for a time during the crack epidemic, has become far more livable and secure. These gains are worth a great deal, perhaps even as much as the vast human and financial costs of mass incarceration. But prisons are often given far too much credit for what has occurred.

The general view that crime is suppressed by putting more people behind bars is supported by a commonsense argument: People who are in prison can't commit crimes against those who are not. It would indeed be surprising if locking up so many didn't have some effect on crime. But even a casual look at the statistics challenges the view that prison trends deserve all or most of the credit for the crime drop. A look at three recent periods (see Table 1) makes it clear that the crime decline of the 1990s did coincide with a large increase in the prison population. But the large crime increase during the preceding period coincided with an even bigger jump in imprisonment, and incarcerations rates continued to climb after 2000 even though crime rates were relatively static. (Robbery is a good indicator of violent crime generally, and follows the same pattern as the murder rate during the period 1991-2000.) If the incarceration surge of the 1990s gets credit for the retreat of crime, then the surge that occurred between 1984 and 1991 ought to get the blame for the *increase* in robberies in that period. Clearly, that doesn't make sense. The point is that we can't learn much from such simplistic comparisons.

Table 1. Incarceration and Crime Rates, 1984-2008

	Prisoners per 100,000 people	Robbery rate
1984-1991	+ 66%	+33%
1991-2000	+ 53	−47
2000-2008	+ 5	0

There are other reasons to question the size of the impact of putting more people behind bars. As Franklin Zimring, a law professor at the University of California, Berkeley, has pointed out, Canada experienced a drop in crime during the 1990s similar to what the United States saw, but without any notable expansion in its prison population. Of course, Canadians do not make an ideal control group for Americans because too many other variables are different to the north, but the general similarity in crime trends for the two countries is nonetheless worth remarking upon. In fact, the crime drop remains an enigma — and, seemingly, a miracle. It was completely unexpected. No expert (or anyone else we know of) predicted it. And now, faced with the fact that this new world of low crime rates is real and has staying power, criminologists have been scrambling to explain it. This is not just an instance of Monday morning quarterbacking. The stakes are high, since the "winning" explanation is bound to influence policy.

In the social sciences, it's usually difficult to provide a satisfactory analysis of past national social and economic trends. There is only one observation — a particular historical trajectory such as the decline in crime — and numerous plausible explanations. There is no way of knowing how that trajectory would have been altered if, say, one of the factors cited as a possible explanation had been removed from the mix. In the case of the decline in crime in the 1990s, there are several possible explanations. In addition to the big increase in the incarceration rate, there were significant expansions of police budgets and an easing of gang wars over the lucrative crack trade. Other pressures, such as a large increase in children born to unmarried women and the growth of income inequality, probably pushed in the other direction, fostering an increase in crime. It's nearly impossible to sort out the impact of these different forces.

Thinking up possible explanations for the crime drop can be a sort of parlor game for social scientists. Why not finger the popularity of hip-hop clothes such as baggy pants, which might impede fashionable, young would-be criminals who have to keep one hand on their waistbands. Or what about the obesity epidemic, which might be weighing against the commission of certain active crimes? Or the pervasive video games that serve as a pacifier for the bored and disaffected? The point is that if we're looking for a way forward, historical trends in American life are unlikely to provide much guidance.

Fortunately it's sometimes possible to isolate and measure the effects of a particular policy, especially if it has been tried in different times and places and a natural control group exists. That is the case with three crime control proposals that deserve serious attention now.

In today's labor market, people who don't have high school diplomas have terrible job prospects and very little to lose in economic terms, so it's not surprising that two-thirds of the inmates in state prisons are high school dropouts. In about half the states it's legal to drop out of school at age 16, but between the 1960s and '80s some states increased their minimum age to 17 or 18. Those changes provide a natural experiment in the effects of extra schooling on crime. Economists Lance Lochner of the University of Western Ontario and Enrico Moretti of the University of California, Berkeley, found that people in the birth cohorts that were forced to stay in school longer had lower crime and incarceration rates as adults than their predecessors did. One extra year of high school reduced arrest rates for young men by about 11 percent. It's not clear what caused this improvement — everything from better economic prospects to the influence of a more salutary peer group could be a factor — but it is a remarkable finding that has been confirmed by similar studies in Britain and Italy.

At a time when state budgets are under severe strain, an increase in mandatory school attendance would be a huge burden. But a lot of additional money for schools could be usefully pared out of the states' prison budgets. Imagine that prison sentences were cut back to what they averaged in, say, 1984. That would reduce the size of the prison population by about 400,000 people while yielding little increase in crime. (The best estimate is that longer prison terms account for about a third of the increase in the nation's prison population.) Spending on corrections would decline by about $12 billion, enough to fund an additional 1 million students per year.

It goes without saying that the extra schooling would have a range of positive effects beyond crime reduction. People who earn high school diplomas enjoy better health, improved employment prospects and greater success in forming families. The same can't be said about those who serve longer prison terms.

Our economics-based "crime of choice" framework also invites consideration of things that can be done on the other side of the ledger, by reducing criminal opportunity. That brings us to our second proposal. One of the most underappreciated developments in crime prevention is the rise of various kinds of private self-protection, from anti-car theft technology to new forms of community organization.

For many youths, the choice to commit a crime such as shoplifting or robbery is strongly influenced by how many opportunities they see and how lucrative these opportunities appear to be. Private self-protection measures give them a shorter and less appealing menu. Uniforms by themselves tend to restrain vagrant appetites. The ranks of private security guards in the United States have been growing rapidly — at more than 1 million, they now outnumber police officers. The move toward a cashless economy has made robbery less lucrative, and burglars increasingly must contend with sophisticated alarms on houses. Technological change has also helped. High-tech devices on new vehicles that make starting the engine without the key almost impossible, along with hidden GPS

tracking devices, get much of the credit for sharp declines in vehicle theft. There were fewer car thefts in 2008 than there were 20 years earlier. All of these efforts have the nice effect of taking the profit out of crime without resorting to punishment.

> One extra year of high school reduced arrest rates for young men by about 11 percent.

An innovative form of self-protection that deserves special note is the business improvement district (BID). BIDs are relatively new, usually established as nonprofit organizations in downtown commercial areas by merchants and property owners who aim to make their neighborhoods "clean" and "safe" — two words that are repeated like mantras in the world of BIDs. The city government's role is chiefly to provide the organization with the authority to collect fees from local businesses. There are more than 1,000 BIDs in American cities, and they are starting to appear in Europe as well. The Hollywood Entertainment BID in California was one of the pioneers in the 1990s. It employs armed private security officers, usually retired law-enforcement officers, who patrol the Hollywood district seven evenings a week, accomplishing a great deal simply by being a presence. They keep an eye on potential troublemakers and get to know the local cast of characters. The BID has also installed eight closed-circuit television cameras for the Los Angeles Police Department to use. All told, the

organization spends a little more than $1 million a year on private security, approximately half of its operating budget.

BIDs have been very effective at reducing crime. A study by one of us (Philip J. Cook) carried out with John McDonald of the University of Pennsylvania found that BIDs cut crime and its associated costs by huge amounts. Every additional $10,000 a BID spent reduced the social costs of robbery by roughly $150,000, and of assault by $44,000. It wasn't just the number of crimes that dropped, but the number of arrests as well. Moreover, there was no evidence that crime was displaced into nearby neighborhoods.

Our third proposal zeroes in on improving the quality of individuals' decision making rather than changing the options confronting them. It's obvious that in considering criminal opportunities, such as whether to break a beer bottle over the head of the obnoxious Yankee fan on the next barstool, people often make foolish, impulsive choices. There are many reasons for that — hormones, immaturity, stress — but surely one of the most important is intoxication. Public policies that reduce alcohol abuse are a pretty obvious crime prevention measure. During the Euro 2000 soccer championships, the mayor of the Dutch host city of Eindhoven ordered the city's bars and restaurants to serve only half-strength beer, hoping to stave off violence by Britain's notorious soccer hooligans. The city remained peaceful for the most part. The next week the games shifted to Belgium, where the beer was full strength and free flowing, and the British fans resumed their violent ways.

Many studies show that alcohol is a significant factor in various kinds of

America's next war on crime must look at the full spectrum of solutions and pay special attention to giving those people who are most likely to turn to crime the skills and incentives to make a better choice.

crime. Victim reports suggest that about one-third of those who commit rapes and other sex crimes and one-quarter of those who commit assaults have been drinking. One straightforward way to reduce this sort of crime is to raise the price of beer, wine and hard liquor. Raising it 55 cents might not seem like a big increase, but it would be enough to persuade, say, some teenagers not to pick up that second six-pack for Thursday night. Data from a 2007 book by one of us, Cook's *Paying the Tab*, suggest that a 55-cent tax would reduce beer consumption by around six percent. And there would be significant fringe benefits, including fewer auto accidents and more money for state treasuries.

These and similar ideas represent a new frontier in thinking about crime. Whatever one thought of the old formula of putting more and more people behind bars, it is simply no longer affordable. Likewise, the old debate between hard and soft approaches to crime has been exhausted. The line between those false extremes is being blurred by

new approaches that recognize that we can deter crime by improving people's life chances, and that coercion can in some cases be a key element of such efforts, as with compulsory schooling laws. As in medicine, an ounce of prevention is worth a pound of cure. We must learn to think of programs as various as preschool education and drug treatment as elements of our crime-fighting strategy. America's next war on crime must look at the full spectrum of solutions and pay special attention to giving those people who are most likely to turn to crime the skills and incentives to make a better choice.

This article was originally published in The Wilson Quarterly, *Winter 2011.*

About the authors: Philip J. Cook is the ITT/Terry Sanford Professor of Public Policy at Duke University. Jens Ludwig is the McCormick Foundation Professor of Social Service Administration, Law, and Public Policy at the University of Chicago.

NCJ 238489

Watch an interview of Philip J. Cook on the economistic framework of crime control: http://nij.ncjrs.gov/multimedia/video-cook.htm.

Watch an interview of Jens Ludwig on the intangible costs of crime: http://nij.ncjrs.gov/multimedia/video-ludwig.htm.

Listen to Philip J. Cook's Research for the Real World *seminar "Economical Crime Control: Perspectives From Both Sides of the Ledger": http://www.nij.gov/nij/multimedia/presenter/presenter-cook.*

Listen to Jens Ludwig and Roseanna Ander's Research for the Real World *seminar "Benefit-Cost Analysis for Crime Policy": http://www.nij.gov/nij/multimedia/presenter/presenter-ander-ludwig.*

The National Institute of Justice is the research, development and evaluation agency of the U.S. Department of Justice. NIJ's mission is to advance scientific research, development and evaluation to enhance the administration of justice and public safety.

The National Institute of Justice is a component of the Office of Justice Programs, which also includes the Bureau of Justice Assistance; the Bureau of Justice Statistics; the Community Capacity Development Office; the Office for Victims of Crime; the Office of Juvenile Justice and Delinquency Prevention; and the Office of Sex Offender Sentencing, Monitoring, Apprehending, Registering, and Tracking (SMART).

Photo Sources: iStock; Veer; and Maureen Berg, Palladian Partners, Inc.